Creating INNOVATIVE CLASSROOM MATERIALS for Teaching Young Children

Creating INNOVATIVE CLASSROOM MATERIALS for Teaching Young Children

Marianne Debelak

Judith Herr
University of Wisconsin, Stout

Martha Jacobson
Iowa State University of Science and Technology

Harcourt Brace Jovanovich, Inc.
New York / San Diego / Chicago / San Francisco / Atlanta / London / Sydney / Toronto

ISBN: 0-15-515786-8
Library of Congress Catalog Card Number: 80-83752

Printed in the United States of America

Credits and Acknowledgments

Photographs: HBJ Photos by Richard C. Polister
Line drawings: Fred Haynes
The Tortillas recipe (page 56) is reprinted from A Child's Cookbook by Bev Veitch, Thelma Harms, Tia Wallace, and Gerry Wallace. Copyright © 1976 by the authors and reprinted here with their permission.

We would like to thank the staffs, student teachers, and children of the Child and Family Study Center and the Day Care Center, University of Wisconsin, Stout. Their cooperation and enthusiasm made the photographs in this book possible.

PREFACE

While attending an early childhood education conference several years ago, we became aware of the growing need for "hands-on" materials for teachers in this field. Through a process of trial and error and evaluating feedback from university colleagues, we eventually designed and constructed two hundred innovative materials for teaching young children. We began displaying these materials at national and state education conferences. The enthusiastic responses of teachers encouraged us to put one hundred and fifty of these materials into a resource book.

The result is Creating Innovative Classroom Materials for Teaching Young Children. In writing this book, we were guided by requests from teachers who wanted creative, yet inexpensive, materials that relate to children's specific developmental needs. Our response has been to organize the book into subject areas that follow most curriculum guides: art, children's literature, health and nutrition, language arts, math, music, physical activities, reading readiness, science, and social studies. Materials in each subject area are accompanied by easy-to-follow directions, clear photographs, and detailed line drawings where necessary. Learning objectives, related themes and subject areas, and strategies for use accompany each material.

Our detailed introduction is designed to help teachers use each material most effectively. It includes:

1. discussion of each subject area and its use in the curriculum
2. step-by-step explanation of the format for each material
3. advice on how to use, care for, and store the materials
4. sources for materials, especially recycled items
5. extended materials that teachers can make on their own
6. a bibliography of books and films.

This book would not have been possible without the contributions of students at the Child and Family Study Center at the University of Wisconsin, Stout, fellow staff members, and friends and families. Our thanks to all these people and especially to Grace Bahr, Kim Klevgard Becker, Jan Erlandson, Shirley Gebhart, Judith Gifford, Judy Hatch, Margaret R. Haynes, Patricia Herman, Suzanne Burmester McCarthy, Teresa Ries, Theresa L. Schroeder, Karen A. Turek, Sandra Voelker.

Marianne Debelak
Judith Herr
Martha Jacobson

CONTENTS

SCIENCE

SOCIAL STUDIES

APPENDIX

INTRODUCTION

This Introduction will provide you with detailed explanations of each section division and of the format for each material. It also includes suggestions on:

    using the materials

    planning your classroom and curriculum

    selecting appropriate materials

    making, caring for, and storing materials

    sources for materials, including community resources and recycled items

    extended materials

SECTION ORGANIZATION

Creating Innovative Classroom Materials for Teaching Young Children is divided into ten sections, and each is a subject area common to curriculum guides. This organization will assist you in planning your programs. The subject areas are:

Art

Art is an important means to learning since it involves the senses and the imagination. Some of the materials in this section are designed to stimulate a child's artistic expression while others are standard equipment in any classroom's art center. The Paint Smock and the Glue Sticks are invaluable aids because they create order for children who are hesitant about participating in messy art activities as well as for children who are eager to participate in such activities. Silly putty, cooked play dough, and baker's clay are popular art media in many classrooms, and the recipe cards in this section allow the children to make these materials as well as to use them.

Children's Literature

Literature not only entertains children; it can teach them about their world. And extensive exposure to literature through storytelling and dramatization encourages a child's reading and language development. In this section, all the puppets, the Storytelling Flannelboard, and the Storytelling Apron can be used by one child or by large or small groups of children with a teacher. The Pirate Prop Box, Paper Mask Puppets, Costume Boards, and Nylon Masks encourage dramatization of familiar stories. Other materials, such as Stick Puppets, Finger Puppets, and Chicken Little Hats, offer different methods of presenting classic children's stories. In addition, all the materials in this section are designed to encourage children to create their own stories.

Health and Nutrition

Children like to cook, set the table, and engage in other household activities. Teachers can build on this interest to teach children about health and nutrition. The recipe charts and books in this section not only offer opportunities for sensory experiences but also teach vocabulary and math concepts. Using the recipe charts, a small group of children can make snacks for the entire class. Or, using the recipe books, each child can make his or her own snack. Other materials, such as Food Classification, Individual Health Chart, and Emergency Chart, explore concepts of nutrition, personal hygiene, and safety.

Language Arts

The materials in this section are all designed to expand a child's vocabulary. Some of the materials promote specific cognitive-language skills: Zoom Pictures, Describe the Object, Feely Bag, Tactile Box, and Language Experience Charts, which promote description; Word Cards, Rhyming Lotto, and Children's Photograph Book, which promote sound-word association. All the puppets and the Individual Flannelboards will stimulate children's conversation and original storytelling.

Math

The materials included here teach basic mathematical concepts, such as size, shape, matching, classifying, sequencing, set relationships, and problem solving, as well as more difficult mathematical concepts, such as numeral recognition and quantity relationships. A number of the materials can be adapted to practice both simple and complicated math skills. For example, the Teddy Bear Counting and Sequencing can first be used to practice matching and sequencing skills and then used to explore set and quantity relationships.

Music

Music can be a source of enjoyment and can also serve as a vehicle for teaching children about different cultures. The materials in the music section include instructions for making a variety of instruments that can then be used to explore the musical concepts of rhythm, dynamics, and tempo. The instruments are designed to be used by one child or by small or large groups of children. The Instruction Chart for Musical Shakers allows children to make their own instruments while the Instrument-Conducting Cards provide directions for using the instruments. All of the materials in this section can be used with records, songs, chants, and dances.

Physical Activities

Children seem to be constantly in motion, and movement is one way that they learn about their bodies and their relationship to the environment. The materials in this section will help to develop a child's small- and large-muscle control. The large-muscle activities—Beanbag Toss, Ring Ross, Pompon Toss, Balance Beam, Balance Strip, Jumping Hurdle, and Frog Toss—teach children balance, coordination, laterality, rhythm, and body awareness. The small-muscle activities—Lock Board, Shape Pegboard, Sewing Cards, Magnet Maze, Fishing, and Sand-Drawing Box—develop eye-hand coordination and small manipulation. All of these skills lay the foundations for reading and writing. The Tying Board and the Self-help Boards provide practice in buttoning, lacing, snapping, tying, and zipping and thus promote a child's independence in dressing.

Reading Readiness

Reading involves decoding written symbols and comprehending written concepts while reading readiness involves a variety of learning experiences that precede actual reading. Using the materials in this section, children can build reading readiness skills: matching, color and shape recognition, left-to-right progression, visual discrimination, sight-word recognition, letter-sound recognition, and word completion. The materials are designed to be used by one child or by a small group of children.

Science

Science strives to answer how and why questions about the world. Since <u>why</u> is a favorite word in a young child's vocabulary, science can play an important part in your curriculum. The Hearing, Tasting, Smelling boxes, the Memory-Texture Box, the Feely Box, and the Color Paddles help children to explore their five senses. Other materials in this section are designed for nature study: Weather Chart, Plant Sequence Cards, Seed-Planting Chart, Animal Tracks, and Animal Track Cards. Some materials promote learning through experimentation and prediction: Sink and Float Chart, Color Mix, and Which Moves Fastest? Slowest?, while the Magnet Attraction Chart and the Magnet Dowels will help children understand the specific properties of objects.

Social Studies

You can explore geography with your class by using the Map, the Landscape Cloth, the Landforms Box, and the Landform Bowls. The children can follow the changing seasons through the Seasonal Fabric Sort, the Dressing Doll, and the Calendar. Where Do We Live?, Transportation Classification, and Occupation Classification will teach your class about the world and its inhabitants. Use the Landscape Cloth, the Tin

Can Puppets, and the Household Sorting Box to encourage role playing. The Attendance Chart, the Calendar, and the Clock will become integral parts of your classroom.

MATERIAL ORGANIZATION

A consistent format is used for each material.

Objectives

The objectives listed at the beginning of each material describe the educational value of that particular material. You should use the objectives as a guide when selecting materials for specific children's needs and later to assess each child's progress. For example, if a child cannot name colors, use the Four-Color Dominoes to determine if he or she can match colors. When the child is successful in matching colors, use other materials such as the Shape and Color Matrix or the Milk Carton Sort to reinforce the color names.

Themes

Themes are general ideas or concepts to which various materials relate. For example, you could develop a theme of families by using the following curriculum materials described in the text:

Household Sorting Box
Recipe Chart
Wooden Spoon Puppets
Household Puppets
Picture Cards
Big, Bigger, Biggest Board
Occupation Classification

A single material can also be used to teach a variety of themes. For example, the Recipe Chart for Baker's Clay includes these themes:

sculpture
senses
cooking
holidays
shapes
I'm me, I'm special
colors

Subject Areas

The subject areas included in this book cover all parts of the curriculum. Selecting a material according to its subject area will help you develop new learning centers as well as enrich already existing learning centers in your classroom.

Materials

This is a list of all the resources you will need to construct each material. Be sure to gather all these items before you begin.

Directions

These are step-by-step instructions for constructing each material. Refer to the photographs and illustrations for additional information.

Strategies for Use

These strategies suggest how to introduce each material to the children and how to use it with them; how to decide if the material is teacher directed or child initiated; how to stimulate the children's language and thought development while they are using the material; how to plan the appropriate-sized group for using the material.

USING THE MATERIALS

In planning a well-rounded early childhood program, you should begin with a basic knowledge of how young children grow, develop, and learn. Child development theory can help you understand why one child works on puzzles while another practices on the balance beam; why one three-year-old has the vocabulary of a seven-year-old and another speaks in one-word phrases; why children between the ages of four and seven are unable to reverse their thinking processes (they cannot understand that the amount of clay is the same whether it is flattened into a disk, rolled into a ball, or stretched into a "snake"). Familiarity with developmental theory will also help you to plan appropriate materials and activities for your children and will provide a framework for curriculum planning.

In planning your curriculum and your long-range program goals, there are several factors you must keep in mind:

1. Consider the community you are serving to ensure that your goals are realistic. A program designed for children living in a rural area would not be appropriate (or rewarding) for children living in an urban community.

2. Consider the individual children in your classroom. Develop a curriculum that takes into account their special needs, interests, and abilities. Most three-year-olds are not interested in printing words, but painting and drawing will give them practice in small muscle and eye-hand coordination—skills necessary for writing. And children

with short attention spans are more likely to stay interested in painting and drawing (while simultaneously acquiring skills).

3. Build on the children's previous experiences. If you have taken your class on a field trip, perhaps to the zoo, continue to build on that experience in the classroom. Add zoo animals to the block center, write a language chart about the trip, create sticker lotto games using pictures of zoo animals.

Planning Your Classroom and Curriculum

Keep in mind that children learn by doing and through active involvement with their environment. A stimulating classroom, with opportunities to solve problems, experiment, and practice skills, will promote learning and growth. When planning your classroom materials and space, ask yourself these questions:

Is the environment attractive?

Is it accessible to the children?

Will the children be able to move efficiently from one area to another?

Will the materials suggest further ideas to the children?

Will the children be motivated to learn?

Block out your general program by the year/month/week/day and develop a daily schedule that will provide a balance of activities:

independent/teacher directed

practice/discovery

active/quiet

factual/creative

individual/small and large group

indoor/outdoor

As you fill in the details for each day or week, remember to be flexible. The children will always provide you with ideas, so be ready to expand or substitute materials and activities. Anticipate problems, such as a change in the weather, staff shortages, or other unexpected situations, and be prepared with alternate plans.

Selecting Appropriate Materials

You can use several methods to select materials from this book:

1. Use a theme approach. For example, your weekly theme might be colors. Find the materials relating to colors, and from them choose the materials that best suit the needs of your children, your schedule, and your room arrangement.

2. Use a skills development approach. Perhaps you discover that the children need to develop dressing skills. Use the Tying Board and the Self-help

Boards to provide practice in buttoning, snapping, lacing, tying, and zipping.

3. Use materials suitable to the learning centers in your classroom. All the math activities listed in this book would be appropriate for the math area of your classroom. If you do not have a science area make the materials in that section and begin a science learning center.

Making the Materials

1. Set up a work space with a large table on which you can spread out your work. Organize all your tools and construction materials in this area.

2. Set aside a corner of your storage area for anything that can be recycled into a material.

3. Use an opaque projector to enlarge the characters in story books for charts, masks, flannelboards, and so on.

4. Reinforce good habits of capitalization and punctuation for your children by using capital letters to begin sentences or proper nouns on charts, maps, and bulletin boards. Appropriate-sized letter and number patterns of the alphabet and 1–10 are in the Appendix. Cut these letters and numbers out of cardboard and trace them directly on charts, maps, or bulletin boards.

Caring for the Materials

When you introduce the materials in the classroom, teach the children how to care for them.

1. Cover tagboard materials with clear contact paper or laminate. (Use laminate if possible, since it is a less expensive method of preservation.) The plastic coating strengthens the tagboard and allows dirt, paint, or fingerprints to be wiped off.

2. Use felt scraps, tissue, and paper towels to remove crayon, grease pencil, and water soluble paint from laminated materials.

3. Materials made from fabric can be sprayed with stain repellent.

4. When making a puppet, reinforce the seams that will get the most stress. When possible, sew fabric rather than glue it because, after a period of time, glue loses its strength.

5. Paint materials made of wood to make them more appealing and easier to clean.

6. For safety, sand the rough edges of wood and metal.

7. Be sure to repair damaged materials before the children use them.

Storing the Materials

1. Store small materials in manila folders, large envelopes, or boxes.

2. Store charts and similar-sized materials in portfolio envelopes that you can purchase at art supply stores.
3. For easy storage and reference, file the materials from each bulletin board display in separate envelopes. Label each envelope with the bulletin board caption.
4. Use painted cardboard boxes for storage since they are light enough for children to carry. Boxes that frozen chickens come in are especially suitable since they have handles, lids, and are covered with a waxy film that can be washed. Ask for them at the meat department of a supermarket.
5. Six-pack soda cartons (painted) make good carriers for paint jars.
6. For easy reference, store all materials relating to one theme in a cardboard box. Or store all materials relating to one subject together.

SOURCES FOR MATERIALS

Community Resources

1. Volunteers, parents, members of service organizations, and foster grandparents can help you in making materials.
2. Inquire at your local high school for used band uniforms, football uniforms, and other types of uniforms and equipment.
3. Other sources for free or inexpensive materials:

paint stores	grocery stores
restaurants	food-service
wallpaper and carpet	operations
stores	drugstores
telephone company	newspapers
post office	fabric stores

Store owners are often willing to provide surplus materials, and secondhand stores offer reasonably priced raw materials.
4. Auto junk yards are good sources of wheels, instrument panels, and tires for your classroom and play yard.

Recycled Items

Parents are the greatest resource available to teachers. Send home a list of recycled items that you want saved and brought in to school. Lists will vary according to your needs but here are some suggestions:

Paper

colored pictures	wallpaper
illustrated magazines	wrapping paper
confetti	photographs
paper bags	sandpaper
newspapers	cardboard
calendars	corrugated paper
cardboard tubes	cellophane

Containers

appliance boxes	bottles (glass and plastic)
cigar boxes	film containers
shoe boxes	jugs
hat boxes	panty hose containers
egg cartons	tin cans (all sizes)
stationery boxes	jars (all sizes)
plastic berry boxes	roll-on deodorant bottles

Plastic foam

trays	packing bits

Fabric

burlap	leather remnants
canvas	muslin
felt	oilcloth
flannel	rubberized cloth
buckram	fur scraps
draperies	chamois
	upholstery

Decorations

beads	rug yarn
braiding	safety pins
buckles	snaps
buttons	spools
cord	thread
eyelets	knitting yarn
laces	zippers
straight pins	gimp
ribbon	rickrack

Costume jewelry

bracelets	rings
brooches	hairpins
necklaces	earrings
tie tacks	cuff links

Natural materials

cornhusks	sand
cornstalks	seashells
gourds	seeds
pine cones	rocks
reeds	nuts

Clothing and accessories

belts	mittens
hats	neckties
gloves	purses
checkbooks	scarves
shoes	stockings

boots
wallets
socks
skirts
petticoats
coats

sweaters
shirts
dresses
nightgowns
pants
jackets

Floor coverings

linoleum
hardboard
ceramic and quarry tiles

carpeting
area rugs

Metal

aluminum foil
ballbearings
brass
copper foil
pans

steel wool
tinfoil
wire
wire screen
chains

Hardware

brads
hooks
paper clips

tacks
screws
nails

Household items

blankets
candles
lampshades
rubber bands
soap
towels

mirrors
Christmas ornaments
phonograph records
shoe polish
sponges
wooden clothespins

Wood

beads
blocks
boards
dowels

sticks
tongue depressors
picture frames
orange sticks

Miscellaneous

chalk
clay
keys
clock springs
stamps

inner tubes
marbles
pipe cleaners
rope
twine

EXTENDED MATERIALS

1. Create a "take-apart table" with broken radios, clocks, record players, and provide an assortment of tools for the children to use.
2. Cut name tags from oilcloth and print each child's name with permanent felt-tip marker. Cover the tags with clear contact paper or laminate. The name tags will be durable enough to last through the year.
3. Make paint smocks from plain, no-iron children's shirts.
4. Make a puppet stage from a large appliance box. Cut a window out of one side of the box to serve as the stage. Cut a door in the opposite side of the box for the puppeteers' entrance. You can cut a similar window in a smaller box and set the box on a table for puppet shows.
5. Make individual flannelboards for the children by covering 12" linoleum tiles with felt or flannel.
6. Fill 35-millimeter film cases (with screw or snap-on tops) with nuts, bolts, toothpicks, seeds, rice, beans, or stones, and use as sound shakers. They can also be filled with vanilla, pepper, peanut butter, and orange juice and used as smell containers.
7. Use frozen food trays and small tin pans as paint containers. For printmaking, mix your paint to a thick consistency and pour in enough to cover the bottom of a tray.
8. Finger-paint on old cookie sheets and trays. This method keeps the paint in one area and makes it easy to clean up. After the child has finger-painted on the tray, place a piece of paper on the paint, press lightly, and lift to preserve the picture.

CONCLUSION

You are now ready to select and construct materials from this book. Making quality educational materials is a worthwhile use of your time. Remember to be neat and precise so the finished materials are attractive, and take the extra time to make the materials durable. The suggestions we offer will ensure the longevity of each piece of equipment. As you present these materials in your classroom, watch the children delight in learning. This will be the greatest reward for your efforts.

BIBLIOGRAPHY

Anderson, Paul S. **Story Telling with the Flannelboard.** Minneapolis: T. S. Denison, 1963.
Invaluable book for teachers of young children. Contains stories and easily reproduced patterns for making flannelboards. Includes beginning stories ("The Big Big Turnip," "Wee Red Shoes," "The Teeny Tiny Woman"), traditional stories ("Chicken Little," "The Steadfast Tin Soldier," "The Emperor's New Clothes"), and modern stories ("The Lavender Bunny," "The Giraffe Who Went to School").

Boxes. Time-Life Films, 1974 (U.S. Release). (16mm. Sound. Color. 30 min. BBC-TV, prod. $350.00. Rental: $35.00.* [Series: Vision On Series.])
Unnarrated. Film uses entertainment, pantomime, animation, slow-motion, fast action, and performers to show different sizes and shapes of boxes and how to put them to unusual uses. For review of film, see **Landers,** Vol. 20 No. 1, Sept./Oct. 1975.

Chelser, Bernice. **Do a Zoomdo.** Boston: Little, Brown, 1975.
Book of craft and fun ideas from viewers of **Zoom,** television show produced by, for, and about children. Instructions are clear and accompanied by photos. Exceptional book for older elementary children to use on their own and good book for young children supervised by an adult. Ideas included are yarn dolls, bird feeders, sock puppets, pillows, pressed flowers, terrariums, corn garden, tree loom, recipes for clay, homemade paint, and puppet cookies.

Cole, Ann, et al. **I Saw a Purple Cow and 100 Other Recipes for Learning.** Boston: Little, Brown, 1972.
Useful book for parents and teachers working with preschool children. In addition to ideas for verbal games, includes directions for making musical instruments, puppets, costumes, instrument panels, and basic recipes for art supplies. All games and materials designed to enhance reading readiness, creativity, and music.

Collier, Mary Jo, et al. **Kids' Stuff: Kindergarten and Nursery School.** Nashville, Tenn.: Incentive Publications, 1969.
Idea book that promotes language arts, science, social studies, math, art, and music in the classroom. Most materials require only tagboard or paper. Included are jigsaw puzzles, wallpaper puzzles, mystery books, touch and feel books, ideas for creative dramatics, hints for chart making, art recipes, and bulletin board activities.

Day, Barbara. **Open Learning in Early Childhood.** New York: Macmillan, 1975.
All-purpose reference book for early childhood education. Helps teacher to create child-centered

---

* all prices as of January 1980.

environment and to stimulate learning through exploration. Discusses blocks, language arts, fine arts, creative dramatics, science and math, social studies, outdoor play, movement, sand and water play, and woodworking. Provides objectives, suggested activities, and ideas for teacher-made materials.

Display and Presentation Boards. International Film Bureau, 1971. (16mm. Sound. Color. 15 min.)
A how-to film that shows methods of constructing and using variety of presentation boards: felt, hook and loop, magnetic, peg, electric, and a combination of these boards.

Farnsworth, Ruth, ed. **Christmas Toy Box: Cuddly Gifts to Make.** London: Collier/Searle Action, 1977.
Patterns and clear directions for making toys that are safe for the smallest child. Includes stocking stuffers, finger puppets, and vast array of dolls and stuffed animals. Also includes section on toymaking techniques and library of different stitches. Most useful for anyone gathering materials for infant/toddler program.

Fiarotta, Phyliss and Noel Fiarotta. **The You and Me Heritage Tree: Ethnic Crafts for Children.** New York: Workman Publishing, 1976.
Do-it-yourself book with concise instructions for one hundred craft projects from twenty-two different ethnic traditions in the United States. Uses readily available materials, such as yarn, paper, paint, fabric, and eggs. Also includes histories of ethnic groups, lists of supplies needed, and instructions for transferring patterns.

Fiveson, Bob. **The Music Makers.** Universal Educational and Visual Arts, 1975. (16mm. Sound. Color. 17 min. $225.00. Rental: $22.00.*)
Film demonstrates how to use self-made instruments to make music. In story format, describes the process for gathering materials, using reference books, and assembling a xylophone, drums, recorders, and a washtub bass. For review of film, see **Landers,** Vol. 20 No. 3, Jan./Feb. 1976.

Gates, Frieda. **Glove, Mitten and Sock Puppets.** New York: Scholastic Book Service, 1978.
Gates, a professional puppeteer, provides clear and simple directions for making a variety of finger and hand puppets from gloves, mittens, and socks. Includes patterns for monsters, dragons, rabbits, and martians. These patterns can easily be adapted to make other kinds of creatures.

Gilbreath, Alice. **More Fun and Easy Things to Make.** New York: Scholastic Book Service, 1976.
An easy craft book to use with children, especially beginning readers. The illustrations are directive

and easy to follow. Contains about fifteen easy crafts.

Glass. Time-Life Films, 1974 (U.S. release). (16mm. Sound. Color. 30 min. BBC-TV, prod. $350.00. Rental: $35.00.* [Series: Vision On Series.]])
Explores the ways puppets, mobiles, dolls, cutouts, and other crafts can be created with glass. Simultaneous narration in sign language. For review of film, see **Landers,** Vol. 20 No. 1, Sept./Oct. 1975.

How to Do: Masks and Puppets. Educational Dimensions Group, 1975. (Sound. Color. Filmstrips with cassette. Masks: 79 frames. 18 min. Puppets: 83 frames. 18 min. $49.00.*)
Provides historical overview, then gives directions for making masks and puppets out of papier-mâché, paper bags, and other materials. Offers useful instruction techniques for teachers to use with children.

Hutchings, Margaret. **Making and Using Finger Puppets.** New York: Taplinger, 1973.
Contains detailed patterns and directions for making inexpensive, attractive finger puppets. Includes simple drawings and color photos. For a more lengthy discussion, see **Book Review Digest,** 1974. p. 587.

————. **Toys from the Tales of Beatrix Potter.** . . . New York: Warne, 1973.
Highly recommended book for re-creating Beatrix Potter's characters. Includes patterns and clear instructions as well as many photographs. Good book for extending literature into other formats. See **Book Review Digest,** 1974. p. 587 for more information.

Inslee, Joseph W., ed. **The How to Book.** Philadelphia: Fortress Press, 1971.
Geared for use in programs with limited budgets. Includes ideas in a variety of categories: displaying pictures; making flannelboards, storytelling figures, wall hangings, charts, games, musical instruments; and growing plants; as well as some basic craft ideas.

Joseph, Joan. **Folk Toys Around the World and How to Make Them.** New York: Parents' Magazine Press, 1972.
Introduces eighteen toys from various countries, gives directions for constructing them, and discusses materials needed. Provides history of each toy, illustrations, and schematic drawings. Includes dolls, yo-yos, prisoners' lock, balancing and manipulative toys. Also includes a list of where to obtain needed materials.

Karnes, Merle B. **Creative Games for Learning.** Reston, Va.: Council for Exceptional Children, 1977.

Presents fifty games that can be made for children three to eight years of age. Each game is accompanied by illustration, game objective, materials needed, instructions for making and playing the game, vocabulary to be emphasized, and possible variations of the game. Objectives include developing visual perception, math skills, fine motor coordination, language development, self-awareness, and sensory perception.

Lewis, Shari. **Making Easy Puppets.** New York: E. P. Dutton, 1969.
Instructions for making puppets from boxes, paper, vegetables, egg shells, handkerchiefs. Includes suggestions for using puppets and a history of puppetry. Good book for older children, or primary children with adult supervision. For further information, see **Book Review Digest,** 1969. p. 787.

Lorton, Mary Baratta. **Workjobs.** Menlo Park, Calif.: Addison-Wesley, 1972.
From her years of teaching, Lorton has compiled a book of tasks that involve and absorb children and from which they can draw conclusions about the world around them. Tasks focus on developing skills in perception, number-matching techniques, classification, sound and letter recognition, number sequencing, and so on. Each activity includes list of objectives, description of the activity, directions for getting started, list of necessary materials, and ideas for follow-up activities. Tasks can be easily adapted to different levels of ability.

Mandell, Muriel, and Robert Wood. **Make Your Own Musical Instruments.** New York: Sterling Publishing, 1957.
Good resource book for making percussion, string, and wind instruments (such as sticks, rattles, castanets, bells, marimbas, chimes, drums, skin drums), using materials found around the home or easily purchased.

Origami—Free Form. Danree Productions, 1974. (16mm. Sound. Color. 12 min. [Series: Origami Series.] $96.00. Rental $4.00.*)
How-to film. Demonstration of simple origami techniques (diagonal, inside/outside, reverse folds) to make goose, whale, dog, fish, seal, penguin, peacock, pelican, and boat. Primary children can make their own paper sculptures. For review of film, see **Landers,** Vol. 19 No. 1, Sept. 1974.

Origami—Geometrical Form. Danree Productions, 1974. (16mm. Sound. Color. 10 min. [Series: Origami Series.] $80.00. Rental: $4.00.*)
Demonstration and explanation of flap, petal, and fold in making windmill, candy dish, flowers, beetle, tortoise, and dog. Presented so that primary children can follow easily. For review of film, see **Landers,** Vol. 19 No. 1, Sept. 1974.

Palmer, Bruce. **Making Children's Furniture and Play Structures.** New York: Workman Publishing, 1974.
Excellent book for adults who want to build child-size furniture, giant toys, and habitats from cardboard, tripleboard, and fiberboard. Includes information on tools, materials, cutting, making corners, templates and patterns, fastening, sealing, painting, and fireproofing. Simple, clear directions for making stools and chairs, tables and desks, beds, storage units, play spaces, tents and domes, habitats, vehicles, and patterns for various geo-shapes. Only limit is the creator's imagination.

Parish, Peggy. **Sheet Magic: Games, Toys & Gifts.** New York: Macmillan, 1971.
Good resource book for parents and teachers to use with children. Clear instructions and illustrations for making toys, parachutes, flags, and so on. For further discussion, see **Book Review Digest,** 1972. p. 1002.

_____. **Costumes to Make.** New York: Macmillan, 1970.
Diagrams, illustrations, and easy-to-follow instructions for making fifty costumes based on historical, story, holiday, and animal characters. Older elementary children may be able to make them on their own but some knowledge of sewing is required. Resource book for extending literature and dramatic activity. See **Book Review Digest,** 1970. p. 1090 for another review.

Sharkey, Anthony, et al. **Cardboard Carpentry.** Education Development Center, Inc. 1968.
Simple text, well illustrated. Explains how to make classroom furniture and toys from tri-wall cardboard. Includes addresses for further information: price, sheet materials, and tools.

Sharp, Evelyn. **Thinking is Child's Play.** New York: Avon, 1969.
Discusses current research in children's thinking, and includes effective introduction to Piaget's theories. Provides abundance of game ideas to stimulate preschool children's classification and seriation skills. Highly recommended.

Simons, Robin. **Recyclopedia: Games, Science, Equipment and Crafts from Recycled Materials.** Boston: Houghton Mifflin, 1976.
Valuable resource book providing stimulus for invention. Presents ideas, originally developed at Boston's Children's Museum, for making variety of games and science projects, such as water clocks, pinhole cameras, printmaking, and toys—all from recycled materials. For further discussion, see **Book Review Digest,** 1977. p. 1228.

Teacher Resource Library. **The Creative Classroom: Ideas for the Primary Grades.** Greenwich, Conn.: Macmillan Professional Magazine, Inc., 1976.

Book of ideas used by teachers throughout the United States. Includes activities in math, language arts, reading, physical education, science, arts and crafts, and music. Activities are easily implemented with everyday materials. Good resource book for the early primary grades.

Temko, Florence. **Folk Crafts for World Friendship.** New York: Doubleday, 1976.

Clear directions, sketches, and photos for making toys, games, decorations, and masks from countries around the world. Each project has an explanation of its history and present use. Designed for grades six through eight, it can be a resource book for adults working with younger children. Published in cooperation with UNICEF. See **Book Review Digest,** 1977. p. 1309 for more information.

Todd, Leonard. **Trash Can Toys and Games.** New York: Viking Press, 1974.

This book provides ideas for making toys with recyclable trash, scissors, knife, saw, sandpaper, and glue. Can be used by adults and children. Book is divided into seven parts each dealing with a different recycled material: wood, paper, paperboard, cloth, glass, metals, and plastics. Objects to make include skatemobile, clothespin people, periscope, glass timer, and bottlegarden.

Tyler, Mabs. **The Big Book of Soft Toys.** New York: McGraw-Hill, 1972.

Excellent reference book containing patterns, directions, helpful hints, and color photos for making soft-toy balls, dice, bricks, puppets, masks and headdresses, shape toys, toys with gussets, two-piece toys, and all kinds of dolls. Especially valuable in an infant/toddler program.

Wilt, Joy, et al. **More Puppets with Pizazz: 50 Rod, Novelty, and String Puppets Children Can Make and Use.** Waco, Texas: Creative Resources, 1977.

Superb resource book with clear directions and photos for making puppets using recyclable items, such as paper lids, ice cream spoons, meat trays, spools, straws, boxes, sewing trim, soap bottles, plastic cups, milk cartons. Easily made by adults and primary children. With teacher assistance, preschoolers could make them.

Creating INNOVATIVE CLASSROOM MATERIALS for Teaching Young Children

ART

TABLE EASEL

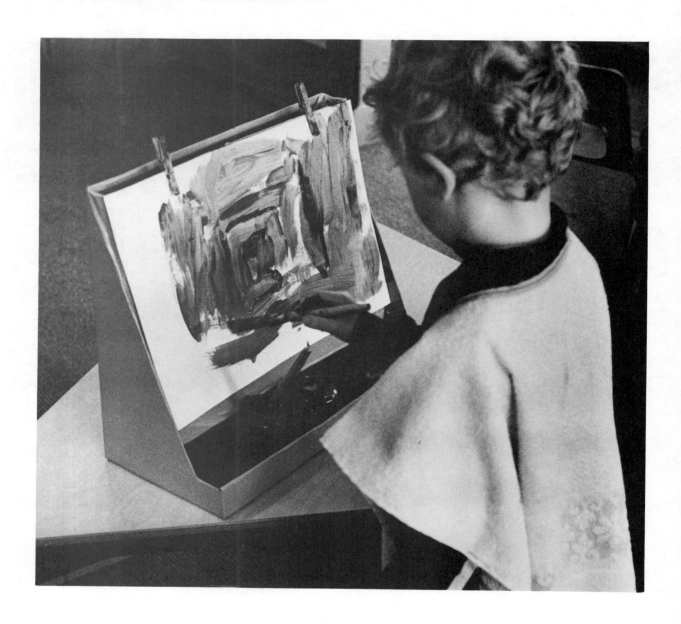

OBJECTIVES   initiate interest in art
encourage exploration of art concepts

THEMES   shapes
colors
I'm me, I'm special
artists

SUBJECT AREA   art

MATERIALS   1 cardboard box, 17½" × 9" × 15"
1½ yd of contact paper (or enough to cover the box)
scissors
masking tape
pencil
ruler
2 clothespins

DIRECTIONS
1. On one long side of the box, using the ruler as a guide, draw a line 2" from, and parallel to, the bottom of the box.
2. Extend this line 1½" around each side of the box.
3. Draw a diagonal line on each side of the box from the top corner to the line drawn in step 2.
4. Using the scissors, cut along the diagonal side lines and along the line drawn in step 2.
5. Remove the cut-out section.
6. Measure the box vertically and horizontally, and cut a piece from the removed section to these exact measurements. Then trim 2" from the vertical measurements of this section.
7. Attach this piece to the original box with masking tape to form the work surface.
8. Cover the box with contact paper.

STRATEGIES FOR USE   Place the easel on table or floor. Use the two clothespins to attach paper to the work surface. Put supplies in the tray: tempera or watercolor paints with brushes, felt-tip pens, crayons, or chalk. The children can create their own pictures. Provide a damp sponge so that, if necessary, the children can wash their easels when they have finished their pictures.

ACRYLIC PLASTIC EASEL

OBJECTIVES stimulate creative expression
develop eye-hand coordination
provide practice in visual discrimination

THEMES I'm me, I'm special
creativity
colors
shapes

SUBJECT AREA art

MATERIALS 2 pieces of wood, 2″ × 4″ × 8′
1 piece of wood, 1″ × 4″ × 8′
2 pieces of wood, 1″ × 2″ × 8′
1 piece of plywood, 12″ square, ¾″ thick
2 pieces of acrylic plastic, 3′ square, ¼″ thick
4 storm window clips
1 box of 6d finishing nails
4 large 3″ bulldog clips (available in stationery stores)
saw

DIRECTIONS 1. Cut the two pieces of 2″ × 4″ × 8′ wood in half.
2. Bevel one end of each piece of wood as illustrated below.

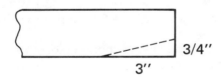

3/4″

3″

3. Cut the 1″ × 4″ × 8′ piece of wood into two pieces, 37½″ long, and one piece, 21″ long.
4. Sandwich the 21″ length of 1″ × 4″ wood between the beveled ends of the 2″ × 4″ × 4′ pieces of wood as illustrated. Fasten the piece of wood at both ends with 6d finishing nails.

5. Cut the 1" × 2" × 8' piece of wood into two pieces, 37½" long, two pieces, 14" long, four pieces, 7⅝" long, four pieces, 3¾" long.

6. Cut the 12" square piece of plywood as illustrated below left.

7. Fasten the resulting trapezoid-shaped pieces of plywood to the edges of the 2" × 4" pieces at their beveled ends, below right.

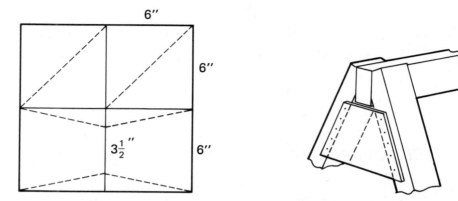

8. Using the two pieces of wood, 1" × 4" × 37½", as the bases, construct two paint trays with the pieces of wood from step 5 as illustrated below.

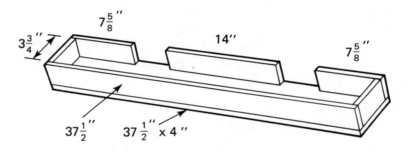

9. Attach the trays to the 2" × 4" pieces of wood 10" from the floor with 6d finishing nails. Start the nails through the 2" × 4" pieces of wood and into the bases of the trays.

10. Fasten the supporting triangle-shaped pieces of wood from step 6 under the trays with finishing nails.

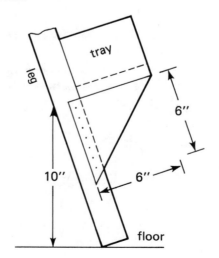

11. Mount storm window clips at the top of each easel leg. These will hold the acrylic plastic sheets in place.
12. Place the acrylic plastic sheets on each side of the easel and tighten the storm window clips.

STRATEGIES FOR USE

The easel may be used by one child or by two children at a time.
Some suggestions for use:

1. Clip a sheet of paper to the plastic (with bulldog clips) and use as you would an ordinary easel.
2. Draw a simple design or picture on the reverse side of the plastic and have the child trace it on the obverse side.
3. Have the children draw directly on the plastic with paint. Press sheet of paper on the drawing while the paint is still wet, rub gently, then lift paper for print of painting.

Children can use paint, finger paint, chalk, felt-tip markers, crayons, or colored pencils. The teacher can use a grease pencil for number 2 above.

The children can clean the easel with soap and water or a commercial window cleaner.

TRANSPARENT
TABLE TRACER

OBJECTIVES	develop eye-hand coordination promote small-muscle development
	promote large-muscle development foster creativity

THEMES	I'm me, I'm special colors
	creativity shapes

SUBJECT AREA   art

MATERIALS

1 piece of wood, 1″ × 2″ × 6′
1 piece of acrylic plastic, 15″ × 18″, ¼″ thick
16 finishing nails, 5d size
wood glue
1 piece of wood, 2″ × 4″ × 11″
saw

DIRECTIONS

1. Cut the 1″ × 2″ × 6′ piece of wood into two lengths, 19″, and two lengths, 16″, and bevel the ends of each piece at a 45° angle (left).
2. On the 2″ side of each of these pieces of wood, score a 5/16″ deep cut down the middle.
3. Fasten two 19″ pieces and one 16″ piece to make two corners. Be sure the grooves are on the inside.
4. Then slide the acrylic plastic into the grooves.
5. Attach the fourth piece of wood (16″) with glue and nails.
6. Cut two supports, as illustrated below, out of the 2″ × 4″ × 11″ piece of wood.

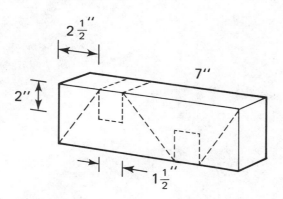

7. Discard the two end pieces. Insert the frame into the supports.

STRATEGIES FOR USE

Place the table tracer on a classroom work table or on the floor. Near the tracer, place cans filled with grease pencils or washable felt-tip markers, tempera paint, or finger paints. You can tape a dot to dot picture, or any other drawing, to the reverse side of the tracer so the children can trace it or paint it on the acrylic plastic. The table tracer can be cleaned with soap and water or commercial window cleaner.

SPATTER-PAINTING SCREEN

OBJECTIVES   foster creativity
develop eye-hand coordination
provide a medium for self-expression

THEMES   shapes
I'm me, I'm special
colors
artists

SUBJECT AREA   art

MATERIALS   1 piece of screening, 10″ × 12″
1 piece of wood, 1″ × 1″ × 42″
1 piece of wood, ⅜″ × 1″ × 42″
saw
16 finishing nails, 5d size
hammer
sandpaper
tempera paint
½″ wide bookbinding tape
toothbrushes (enough for your class)
cutouts of shapes, people, or animals

DIRECTIONS   1. From both pieces of wood cut: two pieces, 10″ long, and two pieces, 11″ long.
2. Using the 1″ × 1″ strips, nail together as illustrated in the photo.
3. Nail the other pieces of wood together in the same way.
4. Place the screening between the two frames and nail them together.
5. Sandpaper any rough edges.
6. Run the bookbinding tape along the seam between the two strips of wood.
7. Paint the wood surfaces (optional).

STRATEGIES FOR USE   Mix tempera paint to a thin consistency. Place a cutout on a sheet of paper and place the framed screening on top of the paper. Dip a toothbrush in the paint and brush it over the screening. The paint will spatter around the cutout shape so that when the screening and the shape are removed, the outline of the shape will be surrounded by the spattered paint.

RECIPE CHART FOR PUTTY DOUGH

Putty Dough

1 cup liquid starch

2 cups white glue

Mix all ingredients in a bowl.

Knead with hands until smooth.

Food coloring may be added with starch.

Store in covered container.

OBJECTIVES   provide a medium for self-expression
practice following directions
foster creativity
provide a sensory experience

THEMES   senses
cooking
measuring
I'm me, I'm special
shapes

SUBJECT AREAS   art
reading readiness
math

MATERIALS
1 sheet of tagboard, 22″ × 28″	mixing bowl
colored felt-tip markers	large spoon
ruler	food coloring
1 cup of liquid starch	covered storage container
2 cups of white glue	clear contact paper or laminate

DIRECTIONS

1. On the tagboard, draw a picture to illustrate each step involved in making putty dough.
   a. liquid starch bottle and one measuring cup
   b. glue bottle and two measuring cups
   c. starch bottle and glue bottle with arrows pointing to mixing bowl (a hand stirring the contents with the spoon)
   d. two hands kneading contents of bowl
   e. bottle of food coloring dripping into bowl
   f. covered storage container

2. Print directions next to each picture.
   a. 1 cup liquid starch
   b. 2 cups white glue
   c. Mix all ingredients in a bowl.
   d. Knead the mixture with your hands until it is smooth.
   e. Food coloring may be added with starch.
   f. Store in covered container.

3. Cover the tagboard with clear contact paper or laminate.

STRATEGIES FOR USE   Gather all the materials for making the putty dough. Set up a center with the direction card prominently displayed so that the children can work individually or in small groups. Once the putty dough is made, let the children experiment with it.

Caution: Have the children wear aprons while making and using the putty dough. Protect floor or carpet.

RECIPE CHART
FOR COOKED PLAY DOUGH

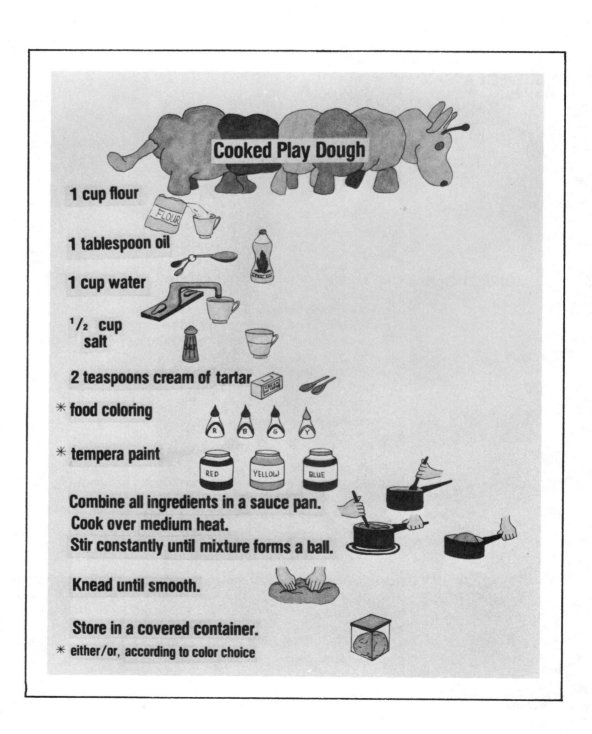

Cooked Play Dough

1 cup flour

1 tablespoon oil

1 cup water

½ cup salt

2 teaspoons cream of tartar

* food coloring

* tempera paint

Combine all ingredients in a sauce pan.
Cook over medium heat.
Stir constantly until mixture forms a ball.

Knead until smooth.

Store in a covered container.

* either/or, according to color choice

OBJECTIVES provide a medium for self-expression
practice following directions
foster creativity
provide a sensory experience
promote eye-hand coordination

THEMES

sculpture	shapes
senses	colors
cooking	I'm me, I'm special

SUBJECT AREAS art
reading readiness
math

MATERIALS

1 sheet of tagboard, 22" × 28"	2 tsp of cream of tartar
colored felt-tip markers	food coloring or tempera paint
ruler	measuring cups
clear contact paper or laminate	measuring spoons
1 cup of flour	saucepan
1 tbsp of vegetable oil	stove or hot plate
1 cup of water	covered storage container
½ cup of salt	

DIRECTIONS
1. On the tagboard, draw pictures to illustrate each step involved in making cooked play dough.
   a. measuring cup with flour being poured into it
   b. tablespoon and a vegetable oil bottle
   c. measuring cup under faucet
   d. ½ measuring cup and salt shaker
   e. 2 teaspoons and cream of tartar
   f. food coloring bottles and tempera paint bottles
   g. saucepan and spoon (do not show heating element)
   h. saucepan on burner
   i. hands kneading dough
   j. covered storage container

2. Print the directions next to each picture.
   a. Combine all ingredients in a saucepan.
   b. Cook over medium heat.
   c. Stir constantly until mixture forms a ball.
   d. Knead until smooth.
   e. Store in covered container.

3. Cover the tagboard with clear contact paper or laminate.

STRATEGIES FOR USE Gather all the materials to make cooked play dough. For safety, this activity is best directed by the teacher. Once the play dough is made, children can, individually or in small groups, create any sculpture they wish or work according to a certain theme.

RECIPE CHART FOR BAKER'S CLAY

Baker's Clay

4 cups flour

1 ½ cups water

1 cup salt

Mix all ingredients in a bowl.

Knead dough 5 to 10 minutes.

Roll out dough to ¼ thickness

Cut with decorative cookie cutters. Make hole at top.

Bake at 250° for 2 hours or until hard.

When cool, paint and then spray with clear varnish.

Makes great Christmas decorations to hang on trees.

OBJECTIVES provide a medium for self-expression
foster creativity
practice following directions
promote eye-hand coordination

THEMES sculpture
senses
cooking
holidays
shapes
I'm me, I'm special
colors

SUBJECT AREAS art
reading readiness
math

MATERIALS

1 sheet of tagboard, 22″ × 28″	rolling pin
colored felt-tip markers	yarn, string, or ribbon
ruler	scissors
clear contact paper or laminate	cookie cutters
4 cups of flour	timer
1½ cups of water	paint and paintbrushes
1 cup of salt	pencil
measuring cups	aerosol can of clear varnish
mixing bowl	cookie sheets
large spoon	

DIRECTIONS

1. Using the materials listed above, make a recipe chart like the ones on pages 12–14. Draw each step and print the corresponding direction next to it.
   a. Mix all ingredients in a bowl.
   b. Knead dough for 5 to 10 minutes.
   c. Roll out the dough to ¼″ thickness.
   d. Cut with decorative cookie cutters.
   e. Use the pencil to make a hole at the top of each cutout.
   f. Place cutouts on the cookie sheets and bake at 250° F for two hours or until hard.
   g. When cool, paint and then spray with clear varnish.
2. Cover the tagboard with clear contact paper or laminate.

STRATEGIES FOR USE Gather all the materials to make baker's clay. For safety, and because of the complexity of the recipe, it is best for you to direct this activity. Display the recipe chart so the children can refer to it while making the clay. Once the clay shapes are painted and sprayed, thread yarn, string, or ribbon through the hole so that shapes can be hung on a tree (for Christmas), in a window, or from the ceiling.

PAINTER'S SMOCK

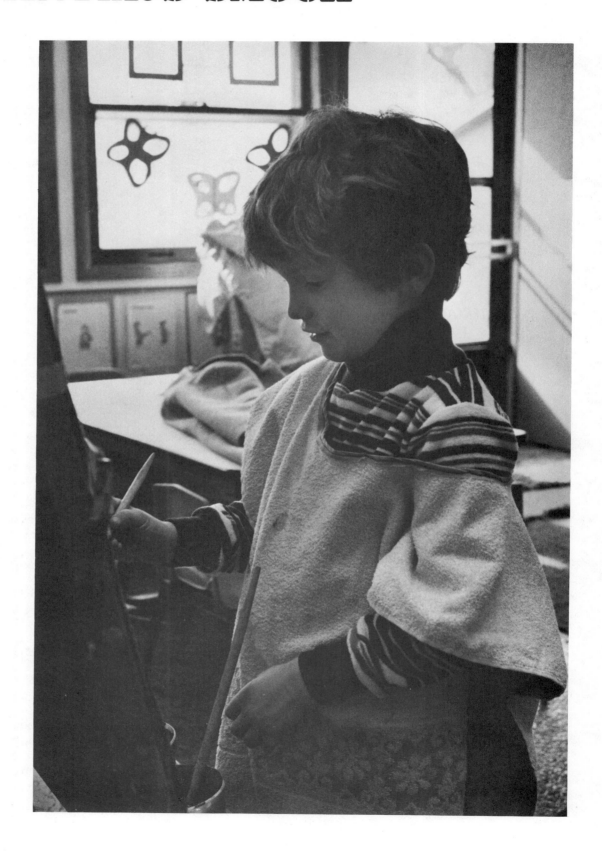

OBJECTIVE practice daily living skills

THEMES shapes
colors
I'm me, I'm special
cooking

SUBJECT AREAS art
health and nutrition

MATERIALS bath towels, 22" × 44" (as many as you need for your class)
wide, doublefold bias tape (in a color to match the towel if desired)
½" elastic (2 strips, 4" long, per smock)
thread that matches the color of the towel
sewing machine
scissors

DIRECTIONS
1. Fold the towel in half.
2. On the fold, cut a hole large enough to fit over a child's head.
3. Finish neckline by sewing on bias tape.
4. Sew each 4" strip of elastic 10" down from the fold, to connect both sides.

STRATEGIES FOR USE Children can wear the smock when painting, cooking, or when involved in any activity that might be messy.

GLUE STICKS

OBJECTIVES encourage eye-hand coordination
explore the various tools that can be used with art media

THEMES I'm me, I'm special
artists
sculpture

SUBJECT AREA art

MATERIALS 1½ yd of netting
10 wooden ice-cream sticks
10 rubber bands
scissors

DIRECTIONS 1. Cut ten pieces of netting, 12" square.
2. Wrap each piece of netting around one end of an ice-cream stick, doubling and overlapping the netting.
3. Secure the netting to the stick with a rubber band.

STRATEGIES FOR USE The children can use the glue sticks when making collages, sculptures, or mobiles. The netting prevents the glue from dripping and makes it more manageable for children to use.

CHILDREN'S

LITERATURE

PAPER MASK PUPPETS

OBJECTIVES
promote verbal expression
foster social skills
encourage creative expression
develop eye-hand coordination
encourage dramatic skills

THEMES
stories
Halloween

SUBJECT AREAS
children's literature
language arts
reading readiness

MATERIALS
colored construction paper
felt-tip markers
clear contact paper or laminate
stapler
scissors

DIRECTIONS
1. Draw patterns or use an opaque projector (if available) to trace characters from a favorite story onto construction paper.
2. Draw facial features with felt-tip markers.
3. Cover the mask with clear contact paper or laminate.
4. Cut out holes for eyes.
5. Staple the top right-hand corner and the top left-hand corner together so that the mask will fit over a child's head.

STRATEGIES FOR USE
Encourage the children to retell their favorite stories from books and to create their own stories and masks to suit the stories. You can also use the mask to illustrate your own storytelling.

HAND PUPPETS

OBJECTIVES
promote verbal expression
foster social skills
foster dramatic skills
encourage creative expression
develop eye-hand coordination

THEMES
puppets
books
storytelling

SUBJECT AREAS
children's literature
reading readiness
language arts

MATERIALS
fur, fabric, or felt (large pieces for bodies, small pieces for features)
2 movable plastic eyes or pompons
scissors
needle and thread (or sewing machine if available)
glue
storybooks (characters to be used as models for puppets)

DIRECTIONS
1. Draw a pattern or use an opaque projector (if available) to trace figures for desired characters. (See basic pattern below.)
2. Cut out and sew front and back of the character's body together.
3. Trim fabric close to the sewn edge and then turn the figure inside out.
4. Sew or glue on the facial features.
5. Cut, sew, and stuff a small half circle of material for a nose (optional).

STRATEGIES FOR USE
The puppet center should contain a variety of unusual puppets. Each child may use the puppets by himself or herself or with other children in small groups. You can also use them to introduce group time or story time.

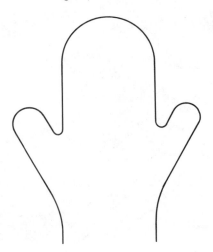

PLASTIC FOAM PUPPETS

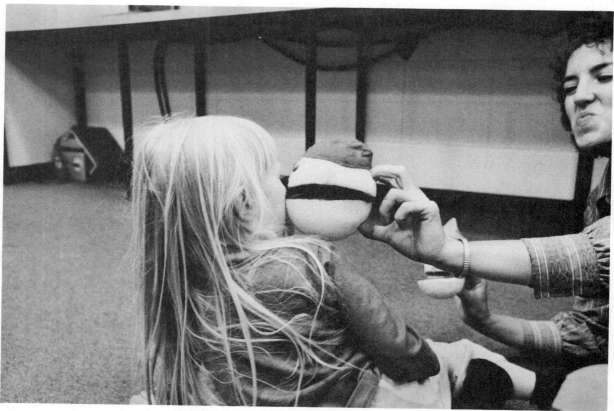

OBJECTIVES   promote verbal expression
foster social skills
encourage creative expression
develop eye-hand coordination
promote dramatic expression

THEMES   puppets   storytelling
books

SUBJECT AREAS   children's literature
language arts
reading readiness

MATERIALS   5" plastic foam ball
1" plastic foam ball
felt scraps for puppet's mouth, tongue, and ears (in appropriate colors)
paint
2 movable plastic eyes
12 thick pipe cleaners, 1½" long (or heavy yarn)
stapler
glue
scissors
knife or single-edge razor blade

DIRECTIONS
1. Cut the 5" plastic foam ball in half with the knife or the single-edge razor blade.
2. Paint the halves any color.
3. Cut one piece of felt large enough to cover both flat surfaces of the halves and glue it to the surfaces. The felt will serve as a hinge for the mouth of the puppet.
4. Cut a pink piece of felt for the tongue and glue in place.
5. Cut holes in the back of the puppet's head for thumb and two fingers.
6. Cut out a pair of felt ears and staple them to the puppet's head.
7. Glue on a 1" plastic foam ball for the nose and glue on the movable eyes.
8. For hair, stick pipe cleaners into the top of the puppet's head (or glue on yarn pieces).
9. You can make a sleeve from felt scraps to cover your arm.

STRATEGIES FOR USE   Introduce the puppet to the class. After the puppet has captured the children's attention, they can use it to tell familiar stories or to create their own stories that can be performed in a puppet theatre.

FINGER PUPPETS

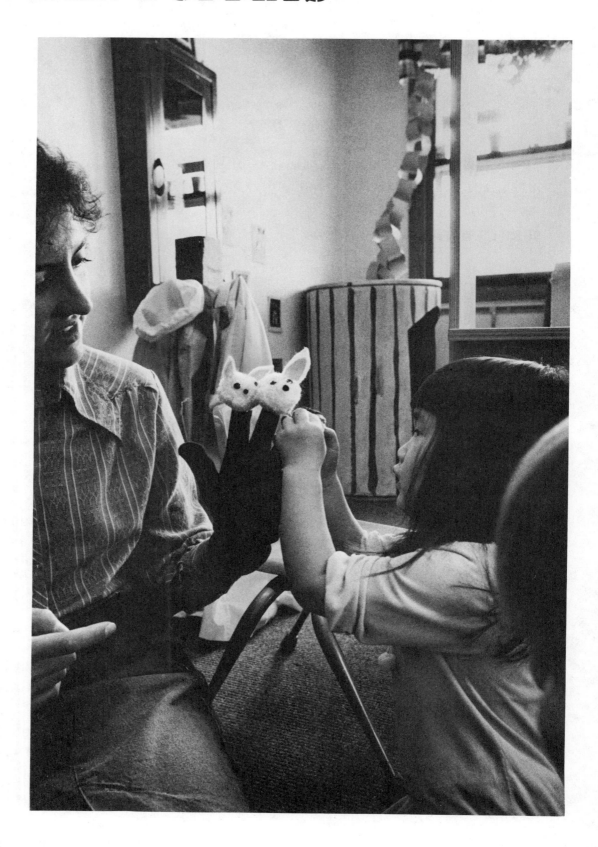

OBJECTIVES develop language competence promote dramatic expression
encourage creative expression develop small-muscle coordination

THEMES puppets theatre
storytelling emotions

SUBJECT AREAS children's literature
language arts

MATERIALS 1 cotton glove (right or left hand)
5 Velcro strips, 1″ × 1″ (can be purchased at fabric store)
2″ pompons (as many as you wish)
felt scraps
movable plastic eyes
scissors
glue
needle and thread

DIRECTIONS
1. Trace and cut out features such as ears, nose, mouth, hair.
2. Glue features onto each pompon.
3. Glue two strips of Velcro to the back of each pompon.
4. Sew two strips of Velcro to fingertips of the glove.

STRATEGIES FOR USE The finger puppets can be used with individual children or with small groups of children. Different sets of pompon figures can be made to represent characters in favorite stories or to represent various emotions. The advantage of this type of puppet is that only one glove is needed since the figures are interchangeable.

STICK PUPPETS

OBJECTIVES   promote verbal expression
foster social involvement
encourage creative expression
stimulate dramatic expression
strengthen sequencing skills

THEMES   theatre
storytelling
puppets

SUBJECT AREAS   children's literature
language arts
art

MATERIALS   sheets of tagboard
fur, fabric, or felt scraps
2 movable plastic eyes (optional)
clear contact paper or laminate
glue
felt-tip markers
scissors
stapler
tongue depressors, ice-cream sticks, or paint-stirring sticks

DIRECTIONS
1. Cut figures of favorite story characters out of tagboard.
2. Draw facial features with felt-tip markers.
3. Cover figures with clear contact paper or laminate.
4. Cut out clothing and hair from fur, fabric, or felt scraps and glue on to the tagboard figures.
5. Attach the figures to sticks with glue or staples.

STRATEGIES FOR USE   Supply the children with a variety of stick puppets and encourage them to retell their favorite stories or create their own stories. The children may enjoy designing and making their own puppets. You can also use the puppets for your own story-telling props.

CAN AND PAPER ROLL PUPPETS

OBJECTIVES   foster language development
stimulate dramatization
promote social involvement
stimulate creativity

THEMES   puppets
communication

SUBJECT AREAS   children's literature
language arts
social studies

MATERIALS   empty orange juice cans
empty paper rolls
felt, fabric, tinfoil, sequins, and yarn
felt-tip markers
glue
scissors

DIRECTIONS
1. Cover juice cans and paper rolls with felt.
2. Decorate the cans and rolls with yarn, tinfoil, felt, sequins, and fabric so that they resemble the desired characters.

STRATEGIES FOR USE   The puppets can be used by small groups of children, one child, or an adult to tell a story. To extend the activity, use them with a puppet stage.

HAND FLANNELBOARD

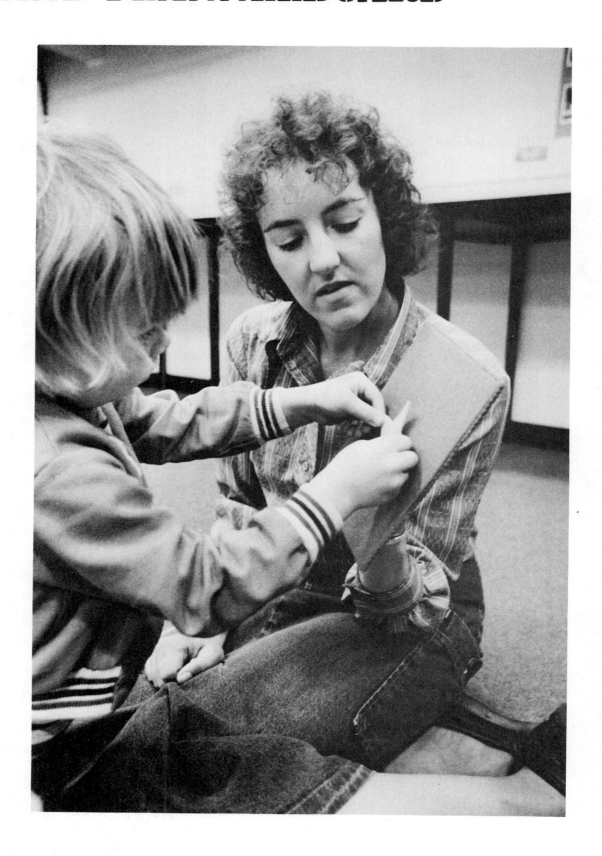

OBJECTIVES	promote verbal expression
	encourage interest in stories
	enhance sequencing skills

| THEMES | storytelling |
| | nursery rhymes |

| SUBJECT AREAS | children's literature |
| | language arts |

MATERIALS	1 piece of tagboard, 6" × 8"
	2 pieces of felt or solid color fabric, 17" × 17" and 6" × 7"
	needle and thread
	sewing machine
	scissors or pinking shears
	felt figures or pictures from children's storybooks that have been backed in felt

DIRECTIONS

1. Wrap the 17" × 17" piece of felt around the tagboard and sew along the edges of the three open sides.
2. Take the 6" × 7" piece of felt and sew it to the board along three edges (to form a pocket on the back of the board).
3. Trim excess fabric along the stitch lines.

STRATEGIES FOR USE

Use this flannelboard with one child or a small group of children. You or one of the children place a hand in the pocket to hold the board upright. The felt story figures will adhere to the board.

You can use this flannelboard with small groups of children to help teach concepts of colors, numbers, letters, and shapes.

STORYTELLING
FLANNELBOARD

OBJECTIVES promote verbal expression
foster social skills
develop sequencing skills

THEMES storytelling
books

SUBJECT AREAS children's literature   art
language arts   reading readiness

MATERIALS 1 sheet of plastic foam or cardboard, 17½" × 27"
2 pieces of felt, 19½" × 29"
1 piece of felt, 5" × 19½"
yarn
needle and thread (or sewing machine)
scissors
1 large piece of tagboard
felt-tip markers
clear contact paper or laminate
sandpaper
glue

DIRECTIONS

1. Sew a narrow hem along one long edge of the piece of felt, 5" × 19½".
2. Place the unhemmed long edge from step 1 along one short edge of one felt piece, 19½" × 29".
3. Sew a line in the middle of the fabric from the bottom edge of these pieces to form two pockets.
4. With right sides facing, sew around three sides of the two felt pieces, 19½" × 29".
5. Turn right side out and slip piece of plastic foam or cardboard inside. Slip stitch the opening.
6. Cut nine pieces of yarn, each 36" long, and form into one braid. Sew this braid to the top of the flannelboard (on the back).
7. Cut story characters out of tagboard. Using felt-tip markers, draw on faces and clothing. Cover the figures with clear contact paper or laminate. Glue a square of sandpaper to the back of each figure so that it will adhere to the flannelboard.

STRATEGIES FOR USE Place the yarn loop around the child's neck so that the flannelboard hangs over his or her stomach. The child can then tell a story by taking the appropriate figures out of the pockets and placing them on the flannelboard. Or you can use the flannelboard in conjunction with puppets so that several children can present a story together. Children can make their own story figures based on familiar or original stories. You can also use the flannelboard as a prop when storytelling to a large group of children.

STORYTELLING
APRON

OBJECTIVES   encourage interest in telling stories
develop listening skills

THEMES   I'm me, I'm special
families
communication
nursery rhymes
fairy tales
holidays

SUBJECT AREAS   language arts
social studies

MATERIALS   1½ yd of fabric (washable cotton or denim)
3 pieces of contrasting colored fabric, 4″ × 4″
sewing machine
material for letters or pictures
scissors
safety pin

DIRECTIONS

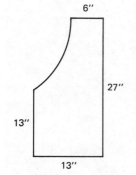

1. Fold the 1½ yd of fabric in half and cut as illustrated.
2. Sew a ⅝″ hem at top, bottom, and sides.
3. Fold over and sew a 2″ hem on the armholes.
4. Cut two strips of fabric, 1½″ × 3′, from material remaining from step 1.
5. Sew the two strips together so that you have one strip, 1½″ × 6′. Thread this strip through the hems on the armholes (step 3).
6. Cut a 10″ × 20″ piece from the remaining fabric.
7. Appliqué characters or letters on this rectangle (optional).
8. Stitch the rectangle 2″ from the bottom edge and 2½″ from the hemmed sides of the apron.
9. Double stitch this piece vertically every 6½″ to form three pockets.

STRATEGIES FOR USE   Put the flannelboard figures, finger puppets, and props in the pockets and wear the apron as a storytelling accessory.

SPONGE STORY CHARACTERS

OBJECTIVES promote storytelling
enhance sequencing skills
stimulate creative expression

THEMES storytelling
art
creativity

SUBJECT AREAS children's literature
language arts
art

MATERIALS 4 household sponges
single-edge razor blade, knife, or scissors
crayons or felt-tip markers
ruler
tempera paint
paper (suitable for fingerpainting)
shallow containers for paint: pie plates, packaged dinner trays, or meat trays

DIRECTIONS
1. On each sponge, draw or trace the outline of a different story character. Goldilocks and the three bears are illustrated in the photograph. The first bear is 6" tall, the second bear is 5" tall, the third bear is 3½" tall, and Goldilocks is 4½" tall.
2. Cut out the story characters.
3. Mix thick tempera paint and pour into the paint trays.

STRATEGIES FOR USE You will have to explain the process involved in this activity to the children. They can dip the sponge story characters into the paint and then print an image on the paper. Some children may wish to portray an entire story or just some key scenes from a story. After the pictures have dried, the children can add finishing touches to the pictures with crayons or felt-tip markers. Or the children can dictate a story to you and you can print it under the pictures. Then these pictures with words can be made into a book.

STENCILS
OF STORY CHARACTERS

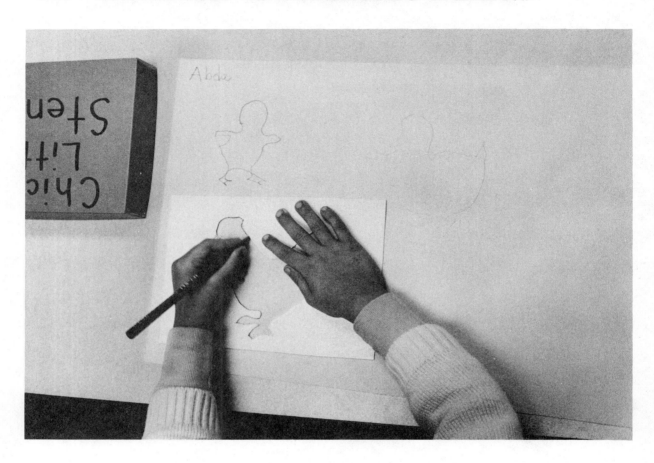

OBJECTIVES promote verbal expression
encourage creative expression
develop eye-hand coordination
develop small-muscle skills

THEMES books
storytelling
puppets

SUBJECT AREAS children's literature
language arts
reading readiness
art

MATERIALS 1 piece of 6" × 8½" tagboard for each story character
scissors or single-edge razor blade
clear contact paper or laminate
cardboard shoe box, clear plastic shoe box, or container of comparable size

DIRECTIONS 1. Trace characters from coloring books or story books onto the tagboard.
2. Cover each drawing of a story character with clear contact paper or laminate.
3. Cut out the story character.

STRATEGIES FOR USE The children can trace the stencils and make their own storybooks. They can also dictate a story that you can write below the tracings of the characters. Or, if possible, they can write out their own stories.
Extend this activity by making the stencils into stick puppets.

PIRATE PROP BOX

OBJECTIVES   promote verbal expression   foster group involvement
                 stimulate dramatic skills   encourage creative expression

THEMES   theatre
             storytelling
             pirates

SUBJECT AREAS   social studies
                    language arts

MATERIALS   1 cardboard box, 24" square (or larger)
                child's shirt (from a secondhand store or the lost and found box at school)
                2 brass curtain rings
                string
                felt-tip markers
                2 pieces of white fabric, 6" square, for each shirt
                1 piece of black fabric, 2" square, for each eye patch
                needle and thread
                scissors
                glue
                stapler
                black and white construction paper
                colored scarf

DIRECTIONS
1. Draw a skull on one piece of white fabric and crossbones on the other. Then draw eyes, nose, and mouth on the skull with a felt-tip marker.
2. Cut out skull and crossbones and sew to the back of the shirt.
3. Cut two lengths of string, 8" long.
4. Tie each piece of string to a brass ring forming a loop. These pirate earrings can then be worn by placing the loop of string over a child's ear allowing the ring to hang near the ear lobe.
5. Cut two pieces of string, 10½" long, and draw through the corners of the black fabric, which becomes the pirate's eye patch. It covers one eye and is tied behind the head.
6. Cut a shape (at left) out of a piece of black construction paper.
7. Cut a 2½" × 12" strip from black construction paper.
8. Staple this strip to each end of the hat.
9. Draw a skull and crossbones on a piece of white construction paper and add eyes, nose, and mouth with a black felt-tip marker.
10. Cut out the skull and crossbones and glue them to the front of the hat.
11. Print "Pirate Prop Box" on the side of the box and use it for storing the props.

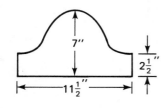

STRATEGIES FOR USE   The children can wear these props to portray a character for story dramatization. Put pirate stories, such as **Custard, The Dragon,** and **The Smallest Pirate,** in the box. Extend this activity by developing prop boxes for other story characters.

CHICKEN LITTLE HATS

OBJECTIVES   foster creative expression
encourage social involvement
develop sequencing skills
stimulate language development

THEMES   hats
I'm me, I'm special
seasons

SUBJECT AREAS   language arts
social studies

MATERIALS   yarn
4 pieces of construction paper, 12″ × 14″ (2 yellow, 1 red, 1 orange)
stapler
paper punch
scissors

DIRECTIONS   1. Fold two corners of each piece of construction paper over and glue down to make a point (bill).
2. At the other two corners, make a 5″, 45°, cut. Overlap the flaps and staple together to make the back of the hat.
3. Punch a hole at each side of the hat behind the bill.
4. Pull yarn through the holes. The children can tie it under their chins.

STRATEGIES FOR USE   Hats are to be used for dramatization. They can be used successfully with small or large groups of children. If you have a large group, make several hats for each character.

COSTUME BOARDS

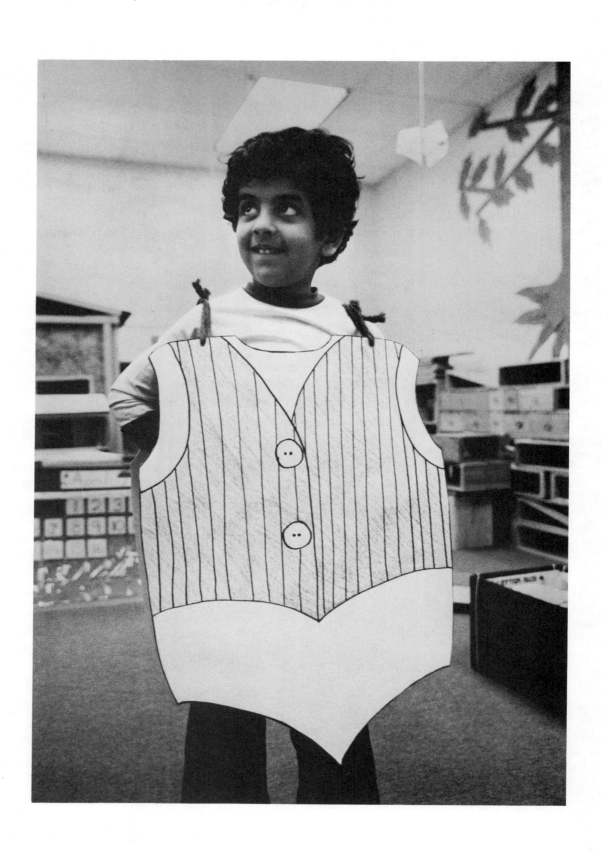

OBJECTIVES   provide a medium for creative expression
stimulate dramatic skills
foster social involvement
promote verbal expression

THEMES   theatre
storytelling

SUBJECT AREAS   children's literature
language arts

MATERIALS   2 sheets of tagboard, 22" × 28", for each character
felt-tip markers
scissors
paper punch
yarn, string, or ribbon

DIRECTIONS
1. Choose a story that you think the children would be able to dramatize, such as "The Three Little Pigs."
2. Sketch the front of each character on a piece of tagboard.
3. Using felt-tip markers, draw in the details of the character's body and clothing.
4. Draw the back of the character on the second piece of tagboard and again fill in all the details.
5. Cut out the body shapes for each character.
6. Punch two holes, about 6" apart, near the shoulder of each figure.
7. Thread yarn, string, or ribbon through these holes and tie knots to secure. Costume boards pictured have 6" lengths of braided yarn with 5½" of slack between boards.

STRATEGIES FOR USE   When the children wear the costume boards, their heads, arms, and legs complete the characters. Costume boards can be used to dramatize any story. Extend this activity by letting the children make their own costume boards.

NYLON MASK

OBJECTIVES   stimulate creative expression
develop language competence
encourage role playing

THEMES   I'm me, I'm special
theatre
Halloween

SUBJECT AREAS   children's literature
language arts

MATERIALS   wire clothes hanger
nylon stocking (or panty hose)
glue
yarn
masking tape
fabric and felt scraps
scissors

DIRECTIONS
1. Bend the hanger into a diamond shape and bend the hook end to form a handle.
2. Stretch a nylon stocking tightly over the hanger and pull end of stocking over the handle.
3. Tape stocking to handle.
4. Cut out facial features from felt and fabric and glue onto the mask.
5. Glue yarn on for hair.

STRATEGIES FOR USE   At Halloween, as well as other times of the year, it is interesting for the children to have a Mask Interest-Center. They can use the mask to dramatize stories and characters. Extend this activity by allowing the children to make their own masks.

HEALTH AND

NUTRITION

INDIVIDUAL RECIPE BOOKS

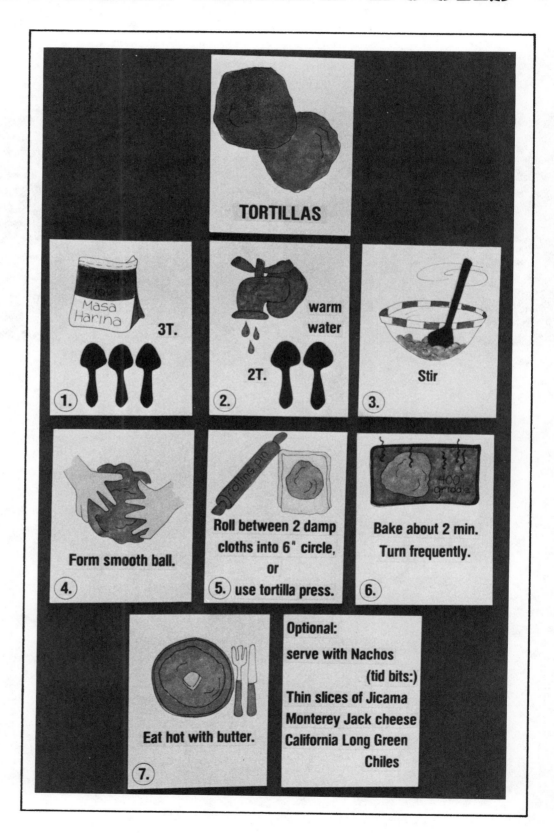

TORTILLAS

1. Masa Harina 3T.
2. warm water 2T.
3. Stir
4. Form smooth ball.
5. Roll between 2 damp cloths into 6" circle, or use tortilla press.
6. Bake about 2 min. Turn frequently.
7. Eat hot with butter.

Optional:
serve with Nachos (tid bits:)
Thin slices of Jicama
Monterey Jack cheese
California Long Green Chiles

OBJECTIVES	develop visual-association skills
	practice following directions
	enhance sequencing skills
	foster interest in different foods
	increase sensory awareness
	develop a sense of quantity
	enhance self-confidence

THEMES	food
	families at home
	cultures around the world

SUBJECT AREAS	language arts
	math
	social studies

MATERIALS	6–10 tagboard cards, 7″ × 9″
	felt-tip markers
	clear contact paper or laminate
	recipes reduced to one portion

DIRECTIONS

1. On separate cards, draw each step of the recipe illustrating the ingredients, their amounts, and the directions. The recipe book illustrated is for tortillas.
2. Write the step number in the lower left-hand corner of each card.
3. Cover each card with clear contact paper or laminate.

STRATEGIES FOR USE

Lay the cards on a table and match the appropriate direction with the ingredient and its correct measurement. Have containers in which the children can mix the ingredients. The children begin with card number 1 and walk around the table following the directions. When they have completed the recipe, they can eat their own portion.

TOOTHPASTE RECIPE CHART

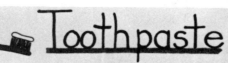 Toothpaste

Place 2 tablespoons  in

electric blender.
Run at high speed until fine.
Add 2 ounces

and ½ cup water.
Blend until mixed.

Add one 16 ounce box .

Blend until all is mixed.

OBJECTIVES   practice following directions
practice left-to-right progression skills
develop a sense of quantity
observe changes in a substance

THEMES   health
dentist

SUBJECT AREAS   health
science

MATERIALS   1 sheet of tagboard, 22″ × 28″
felt-tip markers
label from a container of salt
front panel of baking soda box
glue
clear contact paper or laminate

DIRECTIONS   1. On the sheet of tagboard, print the recipe and symbols as illustrated in the photo.
   a. Place 2 tbsp salt in an electric blender and run at high speed until salt is very fine.
   b. Add ½ cup plus 2 ounces of water to the salt and blend.
   c. Add one 16-ounce box of baking soda to salt and water and blend.
2. Cover the chart with clear contact paper or laminate.

STRATEGIES FOR USE   This activity is more successful with a small group of children so they can all participate. After the toothpaste is prepared, have the children brush their teeth with it. The activity can be extended by adding almond, peppermint, or wintergreen flavoring to the toothpaste.

RECIPE CHART

APPLE SAUCE

1. Peel apples

2. Core and cut apples

3. Put apples in sauce pan

4. Add just enough water to cover apples in pan

CINNAMON

SUGAR

5. Cook apples over low heat

6. Add sugar and cinnamon and eat!

OBJECTIVES   practice left-to-right progression skills

develop visual-discrimination skills

develop mathematical skills

introduce cooking concepts, such as stirring, beating, pouring, measuring, crushing, blending, baking, mixing

observe changes in a substance

THEMES   cooks, cooking

food

families

bakers, baking

who am I?

SUBJECT AREAS   science

math

language arts

reading readiness

MATERIALS   tagboard

your favorite cookbook

pencil

colored felt-tip markers

ruler

clear contact paper or laminate

DIRECTIONS
1. Select a recipe that reflects the culture and interests of the children in your class.
2. Read the recipe through several times until you can visualize the steps, then sketch the steps on the tagboard (see photo).
3. Trace over your pencil drawings with the felt-tip marker and then color them.
4. Print the appropriate directions under each step.
5. Cover tagboard with clear contact paper or laminate.

STRATEGIES FOR USE   Introduce the chart and explain each step to the children. Encourage them to repeat the directions back to you. (They can refer to the chart.) Then prepare the food as indicated, encouraging the children to work independently. Discuss each step of the process.

INDIVIDUAL
HEALTH CHART

	Monday	Tuesday	Wednesday	Thursday	Friday
Did you eat breakfast?					
Did you wash your face?					
Did you brush your teeth?					
Did you comb your hair?					
Did you eat lunch?					

OBJECTIVES reinforce good health habits
introduce record keeping
enhance word-picture association
foster self-esteem
reinforce self-help skills

THEMES my body
who am I?
health
self-help skills

SUBJECT AREAS health and nutrition
safety
reading readiness

MATERIALS 1 sheet of tagboard, 12″ × 16″
felt-tip markers
clear contact paper or laminate

DIRECTIONS
1. Divide the piece of tagboard into 2″ segments, so that you have eight segments horizontally and six segments vertically.
2. In each segment, write a day of the week. Along the side of the tagboard write a good health habit and draw a symbolic representation of it: "Eat breakfast"; "Wash your face"; "Brush your teeth"; "Comb your hair"; "Eat your lunch."

STRATEGIES FOR USE Children look at a representation of a good health habit and mark in the square for each day if they have performed that task. You can make similar charts for learning to dress, learning to clean, and so on.

EMERGENCY CHART

OBJECTIVES
learn how to dial emergency telephone numbers
gain confidence in speaking on the phone
develop eye-hand coordination
practice numeral recognition

THEMES
health
community helpers
emergencies

SUBJECT AREAS
health
safety
social studies

MATERIALS
1 sheet tagboard, 22″ × 28″
1 sheet of paper, 9½″ × 11″
felt-tip markers
yarn
brass fastener
2 empty spools or 2 large beads
glue

DIRECTIONS
1. Draw the outline of a telephone base on the tagboard and then cut it out.
2. Cut out two circles of tagboard, one smaller than the other.
3. Punch ten holes in the smaller circle to correspond to the telephone numbers and letters that you will write on the larger circle.
4. Attach the two circles to the middle of the telephone base with a brass fastener.
5. Cut out a phone receiver from the tagboard.
6. Tie a piece of yarn from one side of the telephone base to the end of the receiver.
7. Glue spools, as illustrated in photo, to the top of the phone so that the receiver rests on them.
8. At the top of the sheet of paper, write Emergency Number Dial 911 (write 911 in a different color).

STRATEGIES FOR USE
Tack tagboard telephone to a bulletin board or to the wall. Children can practice dialing the phone and relating emergency information. Discuss with them the importance of knowing the emergency number. Extend this activity by listing all of the children's telephone numbers and having each child practice dialing his or her own number.

FOOD CLASSIFICATION

OBJECTIVES develop classification skills
emphasize importance of good nutrition
introduce a variety of food groups
enhance eye-hand coordination
develop visual-perception skills

THEMES my body
food
good health

SUBJECT AREAS health and nutrition
social studies

MATERIALS rectangular piece of plywood or chipboard, 20″ × 30″
20 cup hooks
5 library-card pockets
1 sheet of tagboard, 22″ × 28″
glue
pictures of food from magazines
water-base markers

DIRECTIONS
1. Screw the cup hooks into the plywood in a pattern that makes five rows, 6″ apart, and four columns, 4″ apart.
2. Glue the library pockets to the left side of the board, making sure that there is one adjacent to each of the rows.
3. Cut five pieces of tagboard, 3″ × 5½″, to fit into the library pockets.
4. Using markers, label each card with the name and picture of a food group: fruit, vegetable, milk products, meat, bread and cereal, and put in the library pockets on the left-hand side of the board.
5. Mount magazine pictures of food on tagboard cards and cut each card to fit the shape of the food. Punch a hole in each card so that it can be hung from a cup hook.

STRATEGIES FOR USE
In small groups, children can take turns drawing a picture and then hanging it in the appropriate row. For example, a picture of a cracker would be hung in the bread and cereal category.

This board can be adapted to any classification game, such as transportation, seasons, and so on.

TABLE SETTING

OBJECTIVES	develop practical living skills
	strengthen visual-perception skills
THEMES	practical living
	home
	who am I?
SUBJECT AREA	social studies
MATERIALS	1 sheet of tagboard, 12″ × 18″
	felt-tip markers
	plate, cup and saucer (or glass), knife, fork, spoon, and napkin
	contact paper or laminate
DIRECTIONS	1. Draw the outline of a place setting on a piece of tagboard: plate, cup and saucer (or glass), knife, fork, spoon, and napkin.
	2. Cover the tagboard with clear contact paper or laminate.
STRATEGIES FOR USE	The children can help the teacher set the table by matching each of the pieces of the place setting to its outline on the tagboard placemat. After the children have mastered matching, turn the placemat over to the unmarked side, and have them try to arrange the place setting correctly.

TRAFFIC SIGNS

OBJECTIVES	introduce the concept of traffic signs
	strengthen visual-discrimination skills
	develop word-picture association
	practice following directions

THEMES	signs
	transportation
	communication

SUBJECT AREAS	health
	safety
	social studies

MATERIALS	yellow, red, black, white sheets of tagboard, 22″ × 28″
	red, yellow, green, white, black sheets of construction paper
	glue
	felt-tip markers
	clear contact paper or laminate
	scissors

DIRECTIONS

1. Cut out the basic shapes of traffic signs from the tagboard.
2. Use the construction paper to complete the signs, such as stop, yield, caution, slow.
3. Cover each sign with clear contact paper or laminate.

STRATEGIES FOR USE

Post the signs around the classroom. Then introduce each sign during large group time. Encourage the children to use the signs when playing with wheeled toys, such as cars, trucks, and buses.

LAN

GUAGE ARTS

WOODEN SPOON PUPPETS

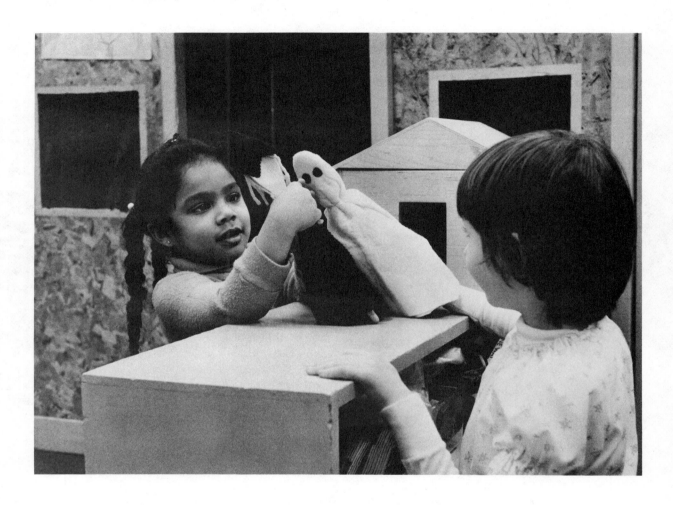

OBJECTIVES   develop language skills
             encourage creative expression
             foster socialization skills
             develop eye-hand coordination
             encourage dramatization skills

THEMES   puppets
             families
             friends
             community helpers

SUBJECT AREAS   language arts
                reading readiness

MATERIALS   various sizes of wooden spoons
             scraps of felt, yarn, and fabric
             felt-tip markers
             scissors
             glue

DIRECTIONS   1. Cut out facial features from fabric scraps and glue on each spoon to create
                desired characters.
             2. Glue on yarn for hair.
             3. Use rectangular or half-moon fabric shapes for clothes.
             4. Tie the fabric shapes at the neck of the spoon with yarn.

STRATEGIES   You may wish to use the puppets for storytelling at group time. The children can
FOR USE   use the puppets by themselves or in small groups of other children to tell familiar
             stories or create original stories.

TWO-FACED PUPPET

OBJECTIVES   encourage verbal skills
promote storytelling
stimulate role playing
provide a medium for self-expression

THEMES   emotions
communication
puppets

SUBJECT AREAS   language arts
children's literature

MATERIALS   2 paper plates
glue
ice-cream stick
felt, fur, and fabric scraps
yarn
felt-tip markers
stapler
scissors

DIRECTIONS
1. On the back of each paper plate, draw the face of a person or an animal. Make the face happy on one plate and sad on the other plate.
2. Glue felt, fur, and fabric scraps on plates for facial features.
3. Insert 1½" of an ice-cream stick between the plates and glue into position.
4. Staple the edges of the paper plates together to form the two-faced puppet.

STRATEGIES FOR USE   These puppets, along with the household puppets (page 78), can be used by a single child or by a group of children to act out stories. A puppet theatre will provide added stimulation. You can also extend the activity by letting the children design and make their own puppets.

HOUSEHOLD PUPPETS

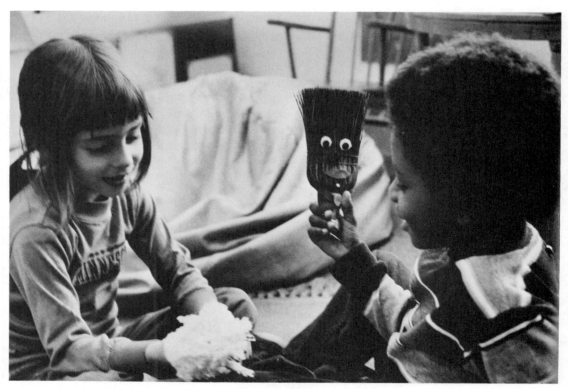

OBJECTIVES stimulate verbal skills
promote storytelling and role playing
encourage social involvement

THEMES puppets
communication
community helpers
families

SUBJECT AREAS language arts
children's literature
art

MATERIALS household cleaning brushes, such as whisk brooms and scrub brushes
fabric, felt, ribbon, and yarn scraps
plastic eyes (optional)
glue
scissors
ball fringe

DIRECTIONS 1. Make facial features and clothing for people or animals from the scraps of fabric, felt, ribbon, and yarn.
2. Glue the facial features, clothing, and plastic eyes onto the household brushes.

STRATEGIES FOR USE You can introduce the puppets during group time. After the initial introduction, encourage the children to use the puppets with a puppet theatre made out of a cardboard box or a discarded television console with the glass removed.

PLASTIC FOAM BIRD PUPPET

OBJECTIVES   stimulate verbal skills
promote storytelling and role playing
promote self-confidence

THEMES   birds   communication
puppets   movement

SUBJECT AREAS   language arts
children's literature

MATERIALS

2 plastic foam balls, 5" in diameter
4 plastic foam balls, 2½" in diameter
6 plastic foam balls, 2" in diameter
yarn
needle
1 piece of string, 55" long
2 pieces of string, 40" long

felt, fabric, fur scraps and feathers
glue
2 dowels, ¼' × 18"
scissors
ball fringe
plastic eyes (optional)

DIRECTIONS

1. Using the needle, thread a 5" plastic foam ball onto the 55" piece of string (for the head). Then add three 2½" balls (for the body). The remaining 5" ball should then be strung for the tail.

2. Make each leg by threading together with yarn three 2" balls.

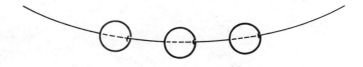

3. Cut the remaining 2½" ball in half and attach to legs for feet.
4. Attach the dowels to each other with string and glue to form a cross (at left).
5. Attach the 40" length of string to each foot and to opposite ends of one dowel.
6. Attach the other 40" length of string to the head and the tail and to the opposite ends of the other dowel.
7. Decorate the puppet with felt, fabric, fur scraps and feathers.

STRATEGIES FOR USE

A child can use the bird puppet by grasping the dowels and allowing the puppet to hang directly down from dowels. The puppet will walk and bob when the child wiggles the dowels. After learning how to manipulate the bird, the child may use the puppet to act out a story with the child supplying the bird's voice. You can also use the puppet to motivate a group story or discussion.

PICTURE CARDS

OBJECTIVES promote listening skills
develop visual-association skills
stimulate verbal skills
promote a positive self-image

THEMES seasons
zoo animals
day and night
families at home
feelings
people I meet
food
housing
health
shapes
families at work

SUBJECT AREAS language arts
reading readiness
children's literature

MATERIALS 4 sheets of tagboard, 22" × 28"
hand-drawn pictures or pictures cut from books or magazines (to illustrate the same story)
felt-tip markers
glue
clear contact paper or laminate
scissors

DIRECTIONS 1. Cut out eight or more 12" × 14" tagboard cards.
2. Mount each picture on a piece of tagboard.
3. Print part of the story on the back of each picture.
4. Number the tagboard cards consecutively.
5. Cover the cards with clear contact paper or laminate.
6. Place the numbered cards in order.

STRATEGIES FOR USE Read the children the part of the story printed on the back of each picture while showing them the picture. After the children are familiar with the story (and if the number of pictures is manageable), have the children sequence the pictures. Then encourage them to retell the story or make up one of their own.

ZOOM PICTURES

OBJECTIVES   stimulate verbal skills
practice prediction skills
develop discrimination skills

THEMES   communication
feelings
self-expression

SUBJECT AREAS   language arts
reading readiness

MATERIALS   magazine pictures of familiar objects, animals, plants, or people
manila folders
glue
scissors

DIRECTIONS   1. Glue each picture inside a manila folder.
2. Cut a small hole in the front of each folder large enough to disclose a small portion of the picture.

STRATEGIES FOR USE   Zoom pictures can be used by pairs of children or by a child and teacher. The child looks at the small part of the picture visible through the hole in the folder and then describes the whole picture. As the children interact with each other, you can stimulate language by asking the following questions:
Tell me what the picture looks like?
What colors does it have?
What shape is it?
How do you think this would feel if you touched it?
What might it be part of?

WHAT'S WRONG WITH THE PICTURES?

OBJECTIVES develop visual-discrimination skills   strengthen word-picture association
stimulate verbal skills   practice small manipulation skills

THEMES communication
adaptable to any theme

SUBJECT AREAS language arts
reading readiness

MATERIALS 1 piece of tagboard, 16" × 20"   crayon, grease pen, or water-base marker
felt-tip markers   tissue or felt scraps
clear contact paper or laminate   scissors

DIRECTIONS
1. Cut tagboard into 16 cards, 4" × 5".
2. On each card, draw a simple picture with an obvious error, i.e., seal with a dog's head, rabbit sitting on a birdhouse perch, girl with a moustache, fish with legs and feet, chicken with a toucan's beak, boy with cat's nose and whiskers, kangaroo with doll in pouch, or giraffe with clown's head.
3. Cover with clear contact paper or laminate.

STRATEGIES FOR USE The children are to look at the cards and then describe what's wrong with each picture. For example, you may ask: "Do all giraffes look like this?" "Tell me what a real giraffe looks like." These cards can also be used by having the child circle the part of the picture that is wrong. After the child is finished, the circle can be erased by wiping with a tissue or a piece of felt.

CHILDREN'S PHOTOGRAPH BOOK

OBJECTIVES stimulate verbal expression
promote storytelling skills
develop creative expression
encourage a positive self-image

THEMES photography
I'm me, I'm special
storytelling

SUBJECT AREAS language arts
social studies
reading readiness

MATERIALS photographs or magazine pictures of people and animals
photo album (commercial or made by the teacher)
ruled paper, 8½" × 10"
pencil
scissors

DIRECTIONS 1. After selecting photographs or magazine pictures of interest to the children, mount each picture on a page of the photo album.
2. Cut the ruled paper to fit in the space below each photograph.

STRATEGIES FOR USE Encourage the children to look at all the photos in the album. Then each child should select one picture to use in telling a story. As the child dictates the story, you can print it on the ruled paper. Then mount the story below the photo in the album. The completed album can be placed in the book area of the classroom for exploration during a free play period.

DESCRIBE THE OBJECT

OBJECTIVES
stimulate verbal skills
expand vocabulary
enhance description skills
develop auditory skills
promote visual-discrimination skills

THEMES
colors
communication
shapes

SUBJECT AREAS
language arts
reading readiness

MATERIALS
2 shoe boxes
yellow fabric scraps (or any color)
white contact paper or construction paper
ruler
felt-tip markers
20 objects, all of the same color. For yellow, use 2 pencils, 2 barettes, 2 sponges, 2 buttons, 2 pieces of felt, 2 pieces of gum, 2 plastic eggs, 2 plastic lemons, 2 pieces of fabric, 2 combs
glue
scissors

DIRECTIONS
1. Cover the shoe boxes with the contact paper or construction paper.
2. Cut two yellow circles from the fabric and glue them to the top of each shoe box.
3. Using a ruler, divide the inside of each box lid into eight sections.
4. Print a numeral from one to eight in each section.
5. Place ten yellow objects (or the color of your choice) in each box.

STRATEGIES FOR USE
This can be introduced to each child or to a pair of children. If two children are using it, they should sit back to back and should both have the lid of the box directly in front of the box, which is tipped on its side. One child (the coder) describes an object and places it on a numeral. The coder does not name the object but does say on which numeral he or she is placing the object. (For example: "Find the yellow object that is long, round, smooth, and which you could write with and place it on number four." The other child (the decoder) listens carefully to the coder, decides which object is being described, and puts that object on his or her box lid on the same number. Continue until the eight sections have objects on them. After the game is finished, the children compare the objects on the numbers to check their skill in describing objects and in listening.

The game may be simplified by drawing pictures of the objects on the box lid. Then the children don't have to recognize the numbers to play the game.

FEELY BAG

OBJECTIVES   identify objects by touch
enhance language skills
foster association skills

THEME   five senses

SUBJECT AREA   language arts

MATERIALS   top of a sock, mitten, or glove
piece of fabric, 9" × 18"
needle and thread or sewing machine
common household objects, such as a fork, a spoon, a spool of thread, a penny,
a toothbrush, a comb
scissors

DIRECTIONS   1. Fold fabric in half and sew the two sides together with a ½" seam.
2. Turn sewn fabric right side out.
3. Fold over top edges ½".
4. Place sock top in opening of bag and sew all around.

STRATEGIES FOR USE   Place an object in the bag and encourage the children to reach into the bag, touch the object, and identify it.
    This activity can be extended by:
1. using pictures of each object and having the children find the object to match in the bag;
2. putting objects in the bag with variable characteristics, that is, hard, soft, rough, smooth, large, small, round, square, and so on and having the children identify them;
3. in a small group have one child look in the bag for the object. After that child looks at the object, he or she gives clues about the object to help the other children guess what the object is.

TACTILE BOX

OBJECTIVES   stimulate verbal skills
strengthen memory skills
expand visual-discrimination skills

THEMES   touch
communication
self-expression

SUBJECT AREAS   language arts
science

MATERIALS   1 shoe box
deep-pile carpet scraps
colored contact paper or construction paper
corn, oats, macaroni, beans (to put in the shoe box)

DIRECTIONS   1. Glue a piece of carpet to the inside bottom of the shoe box and cover the box with contact or construction paper.
2. Place the corn, oats, macaroni, beans in the box.

STRATEGIES FOR USE   The children should use this box one at a time. Each child feels the objects on the carpeting, describes them, and, finally, names each item. The child can be blindfolded during this process.
   One child can feel an object in the box and then describe it to a small group of children. The children try to name the object. The child who names the object correctly then gets a chance to feel and describe another object in the box.

RHYMING LOTTO

OBJECTIVES   develop auditory-association skills
encourage matching skills
stimulate language skills

THEMES   words
sounds

SUBJECT AREAS   language arts
reading readiness

MATERIALS   4 tagboard cards, 8¼" × 10¾"   colored felt-tip markers
16 tagboard cards, 3" × 3¾"   clear contact paper or laminate

DIRECTIONS
1. Divide each of the large cards into eight equal rectangles.
2. In the four rectangles on the left sides of the large cards, draw easily rhymed words (such as hat, book), one in each of the rectangles.
3. On the small cards, draw pictures of objects that will rhyme with the pictures on the large cards (such as cat, hook).
4. Print the rhyming words under the appropriate pictures on all the cards.
5. Cover all the cards with clear contact paper or laminate.

STRATEGIES FOR USE   Distribute the large cards to four children. Place the small cards face down on the floor or a table. The first child draws the top card and identifies the picture. All the children check the pictures on their large cards to see who has the matching rhyming pictures. Whoever has it takes the small card and places it in the space provided. The game continues until one child completes his or her large card or until all the children complete their cards.

WORD CARDS

OBJECTIVES   stimulate verbal skills
develop word-association skills
expand vocabulary

THEMES   communication
matching

SUBJECT AREAS   language arts
reading readiness

MATERIALS   1 sheet of tagboard, 8″ × 10″
20 tagboard cards, 3″ × 3″
20 pictures of different objects from magazines or decorative stickers (pumpkins, animals, and so on)
glue
felt-tip markers
clear contact paper or laminate
stapler
scissors

DIRECTIONS   1. Glue a picture or sticker onto each of the tagboard cards.
2. Print the name of the object under its picture.
3. Cover the cards with clear contact paper or laminate.
4. Fold the 8″ × 10″ tagboard card in half.
5. Staple the corners of this card together and print "WORDS" on the outside. Use as an envelope to hold the small cards.

STRATEGIES FOR USE   You can use these word cards to help the children practice their printing. Provide the children with paper and pencils and have them copy the name of the object that is printed on the card.

You can also use the word cards as flash cards especially when the children have developed word recognition skills. Cover up the picture on the card so that the children can only see the printed word. Then have the children say the word out loud. Uncover the picture to check the children's reading.

LANGUAGE EXPERIENCE CHARTS

🔥 Safety

We learned about 🔥 prevention. We visited the 🔥 station and 👀 many 🚒, ⛑, 👢, and equipment. The firefighters liked the 🍪 we made for them. This was our way of saying "thank you to them. Charlie Brown and his friends taught us the 🔥 rules. We all became 🛡 and checked our 🏠 for 🔥 hazards. We learned the ☎ emergency number. It is 911.

OBJECTIVES promote verbal expression
stimulate storytelling skills
practice decoding symbols and written words

THEMES fire fighters
police officers
the grocery store
caterpillars and butterflies
adaptable to any field trip

SUBJECT AREAS language arts
reading readiness

MATERIALS 1 sheet of ruled manuscript paper, 2' × 3'
felt-tip markers
construction paper
scissors
tape or glue

DIRECTIONS
1. After a field trip, an outing, or a memorable event in the classroom, allow the children to discuss the experience.
2. Print the children's comments, editing them to form a story, on the manuscript paper. Leave spaces in the story for pictures of key words. For example, in "Safety" the following key words could be illustrated: fire, helmet, boots, house, telephone.
3. These illustrations of key words can be drawn directly on the chart or on construction paper, and then cut out and pasted on the chart. Color the drawings with felt-tip markers.

STRATEGIES FOR USE Mount the finished chart on the wall. During large group sessions, read the story encouraging the children to participate by pointing to each word. One successful technique is to pause at the pictures and have the children supply the correct word for the symbol illustrated.

Extend this activity by providing paper, pencils, and felt-tip markers for those children who are interested in making their own charts.

INDIVIDUAL FLANNELBOARDS

OBJECTIVES   promote storytelling
develop small motor skills
stimulate verbal skills
practice right-to-left progression skills
encourage a positive self-image
practice sequencing skills

THEMES   animals   family
colors   shapes

SUBJECT AREAS   language arts   social studies
reading readiness   math

MATERIALS   1 piece of plywood or heavy cardboard, 12" × 14", for each flannelboard
2 pieces of felt, 13" × 15", for each flannelboard
glue
stapler

DIRECTION   1. Cover both sides of the plywood or cardboard with the two pieces of felt either
by gluing or stapling.

STRATEGIES FOR USE   Place the individual flannelboards with accompanying felt flannelboard figures
in the language area of the classroom. Encourage the children to tell their favorite
stories to each other using the boards. The board can also be used as an aid in
teaching classification, alphabet letters, shapes, and numbers.

MATH

FOUR-COLOR DOMINOES

OBJECTIVES strengthen color-recognition skills
enchance matching skills
promote problem-solving skills
foster group cooperation
improve visual-discrimination skills

THEMES colors
games

SUBJECT AREAS math
reading readiness

MATERIALS 30 white tagboard cards, 4″ × 4″
1 set of colored felt-tip markers
clear contact paper or laminate
scissors
ruler

DIRECTIONS 1. Divide each card into four triangles by drawing diagonal lines from corner to corner.
2. Draw a circle in each triangle and color each circle so that there is a blue, a yellow, a red, and a green circle on each card.
3. Cover each card with clear contact paper or laminate.

STRATEGIES FOR USE Pass out the cards to the children in the same way dominoes are distributed. Then place one card in the middle of the players. Encourage the children to take turns placing one of their cards adjacent to the cards in the middle, matching colors. As the game progresses, children may match two or three sides. Extend this activity by constructing the dominoes from any group of four objects or shapes.

NUMERAL-DOT DOMINOES

OBJECTIVES facilitate number recognition
practice matching skills
extend visual-memory skills
develop one-to-one correspondence skills

THEMES numbers
sharing
adaptable to most themes

SUBJECT AREAS math
reading readiness
language arts

MATERIALS 40 tagboard cards, 2½" × 5"
colored felt-tip markers
clear contact paper or laminate
pencil
ruler
scissors

DIRECTIONS
1. Draw a black line across the middle of each tagboard card.
2. Using different color markers for each number, on one half of a card write a numeral or draw any number of dots from 1–10. On the other half of the card write a different numeral or draw a different number of dots.
3. Cover all the cards with clear contact paper or laminate.

STRATEGIES FOR USE The children can play this game like a game of dominoes. Or you can encourage them to expand the activity by matching dot to dot, number to number, or number to dots.

WALLPAPER DOMINOES

OBJECTIVES   develop visual skills
promote eye-hand coordination
foster problem-solving skills

THEMES   colors
patterns
shapes

SUBJECT AREAS   math
reading readiness

MATERIALS   36 colored tagboard cards, 2″ × 4″
9 sheets of wallpaper samples
glue
felt-tip marker
clear contact paper or laminate
scissors

DIRECTIONS
1. From each sheet of wallpaper sample, cut two or more pieces, 2″ square.
2. Draw a line with a marker across the middle of each tagboard card.
3. Glue two pieces of different-patterned wallpaper to each tagboard card.
4. Cover tagboard cards with clear contact paper or laminate (optional).

STRATEGIES FOR USE   Children can utilize this educational game individually or in small groups. Place one card on the table or floor. A child draws cards from the pile until he or she can match one side of the first domino. The game proceeds like dominoes until all the wallpaper patterns are matched. Extend this activity by discussing the differences in the colors and patterns of the wallpaper.

BEAN TRADE-IN GAME

OBJECTIVES strengthen counting skills
develop an awareness of sets
foster eye-hand coordination
encourage problem-solving skills

THEME numbers

SUBJECT AREA math

MATERIALS 75 ice-cream sticks
1 large bag of navy or kidney beans
glue
3 containers
dice

DIRECTIONS

1. Glue five beans on each of the ice-cream sticks.
2. Make five rafts by gluing five sticks with beans onto two sticks, so the bottom sticks run along the ends of the five sticks.
3. Put remaining single beans, bean sticks, and rafts in separate containers.
4. Make a pair of dice following the directions in the Appendix.

STRATEGIES FOR USE This game is best when played with no more than five children. The children take turns rolling the dice. They then take from one container the same number of beans as indicated on the dice. After they have accumulated five beans, they can trade them in for a bean stick. Then after they have accumulated five bean sticks, they can trade them in for a raft.

COTTONBALL GAME

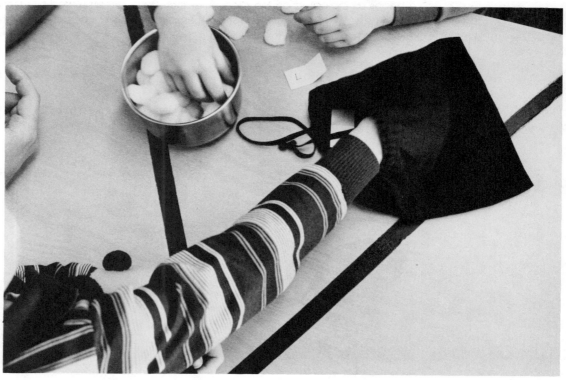

OBJECTIVES
develop counting skills
encourage group cooperation
foster small-muscle coordination
promote sensory skills

THEMES
senses
textures

SUBJECT AREAS
math
language arts

MATERIALS
cottonballs
10 strips of heavy paper, 1″ × 2″
1 drawstring bag, paper bag, or any opaque plastic bag
felt-tip markers
1 basket or bowl
scissors

DIRECTIONS
1. Number the strips of heavy paper 0–9 and fold in half.
2. Place the folded strips of paper in the bag.
3. Place the cottonballs in the basket or bowl.

STRATEGIES FOR USE
The children take turns pulling a slip of paper from the bag, reading the number and counting out the appropriate number of cottonballs from the bowl. You can extend this activity by substituting nuts, wooden cubes, plastic animals, beans, or any other object for the cottonballs. The game is over when all the cottonballs have been distributed. The children then count their cottonballs.

NUT AND DICE GAME

OBJECTIVES encourage group cooperation   strengthen eye-hand coordination
strengthen counting skills   enhance classification skills
foster visual-discrimination skills

THEMES foods
fall
games

SUBJECT AREA math

MATERIALS 6–8 berry baskets or individual plastic containers   paper
$^1/_5$ yd of colored felt   felt-tip markers
colored plastic tape   glue
assorted nuts   scissors
2 milk cartons (½ pint size) or the equivalent

DIRECTIONS
1. Flatten the tops of the milk cartons, making cubes.
2. Cut pieces of felt to fit around the containers and glue on.
3. On one cube, glue a picture of a different nut on each side.
4. On the other cube, glue a number from 1–5 (made from colored tape) on all but one side.

STRATEGIES FOR USE Have the children sit in a circle. Place a bowl of nuts in the center of the circle and give each child a basket. One child roles the cubes (or dice) and takes the correct number of the pictured nut. If one die comes up on its blank side, the players must agree on what happens and the child takes whatever number of nuts is decided by the group.

SHAPE DICE

OBJECTIVES   encourage problem-solving skills
enhance classification skills
foster awareness of sets
develop visual perception

THEMES   shapes
colors

SUBJECT AREA   math

MATERIALS   tagboard
colored felt-tip markers
glue
scissors
yarn

DIRECTIONS
1. Using the pattern in the Appendix, make twelve dice with 3" sides.
2. Using red and blue markers, mark the dice as follows:
   Key: ○ = blue; ● = red; □ = 1 side of a die
   Set 1: On four dice, mark each side with 1 red or 1 blue circle.

   Set 2: On four dice, mark each side with a red or blue square, circle, or triangle.

   Set 3: On two dice, mark each side with the following colors and shapes.

   Set 4: On two dice, mark each side with the following colors and shapes.

STRATEGIES FOR USE
Children can use these materials by themselves or in small groups. Begin with Set 1. Have the children throw the dice, and circle the different sets with yarn. Sets could be: all the red circles, all the blue circles, or all the red and blue circles. Allow the children to make sets as they would classify them and encourage them to discuss the reasoning behind their classification.

Introduce each set of dice as the children master the preceding set.

SHAPE AND
COLOR MATRIX

OBJECTIVES   reinforce matching skills
promote problem-solving skills
extend classification skills
reinforce visual discrimination

THEMES   colors
shapes

SUBJECT AREAS   math
reading readiness

MATERIALS   1 piece of white tagboard, 12″ × 12″
red, blue, and yellow construction paper or tagboard
scissors
felt-tip markers
ruler
clear contact paper or laminate

DIRECTIONS
1. Using a marker, divide the piece of white tagboard into sixteen squares, each measuring 3″.
2. Make blobs of color on the vertical axis of the entire card: blue, yellow, and red.
3. On the horizontal axis, draw the outlines of a triangle, circle, and square.
4. Leave the upper-left square blank.
5. Cover tagboard with contact paper or laminate.
6. Cut out red, yellow, and blue circles, triangles, and squares from the colored construction paper.

STRATEGIES FOR USE   Demonstrate to the children how to select a card and then place it on the appropriate matrix, matching both color and shape. Then encourage the children to play individually or in a small group.

STENCILS OF SHAPES

OBJECTIVES　develop eye-hand coordination
enhance shape awareness
promote size recognition
foster matching skills

THEME　shapes

SUBJECT AREAS　reading readiness
math

MATERIALS　2 large sheets of colored tagboard
clear contact paper or laminate
scissors
ruler

DIRECTIONS
1. Cut the large pieces of tagboard into 6" squares (as many as you need).
2. Cover each piece with clear contact paper or laminate.
3. Draw and cut out circles, squares, rectangles, and triangles from the center of each square.

STRATEGIES FOR USE　This activity can be used with individual children or small groups of children. Introduce the stencils and allow the children to trace them onto paper or cardboard. Some children may wish to make designs or objects from shapes drawn. To encourage exploration, ask the following questions:
Can you trace the biggest circle? The smallest square?
Can you draw a circle next to the square? Between the two triangles?
How many shapes can you make?

NUMBER
JIGSAW PUZZLES

OBJECTIVES   reinforce counting skills
develop number recognition
strengthen one-to-one correspondence
promote visual discrimination
encourage eye-hand coordination
increase small-muscle coordination

THEMES   sizes
shapes
games

SUBJECT AREAS   math
reading readiness
language arts

MATERIALS   10 tagboard cards, 4½" × 9"
colored felt-tip markers
clear contact paper or laminate
ruler
pencil
scissors

DIRECTIONS   1. Draw an object on one side of a card and the number 1 on the other side. Draw two objects on one side of a card and the number 2 on the other side. Repeat through 10.
2. Cover all pieces with clear contact paper or laminate.
3. Cut each card in half vertically with a different cutting pattern, that is, zigzag, wavy, straight edge.

STRATEGIES FOR USE   The children should match the halves of the cards and then sequence the cards from 1–10.

NUMBER BINGO

OBJECTIVES   enhance visual perception
develop eye-hand coordination
promote matching skills
promote number recognition

THEMES   games
numbers

SUBJECT AREA   math

MATERIALS   6 white tagboard cards, 8″ × 11″
1 large piece of red tagboard
felt-tip markers
ruler
glue
scissors
clear contact paper or laminate

DIRECTIONS

1. Divide each card into fourths by drawing lines with a marker.
2. Draw from one to six red circles (1″ in diameter) in each section.
3. Cover each card with clear contact paper or laminate.
4. Cut enough pieces of red tagboard (1″ square) to cover all the circles on the tagboard cards.
5. Make two tagboard dice (see pattern and directions in the Appendix). On one die, mark from one to six red dots on each side. On the other die, write the numbers from one to six, one on each side. Cover the dice with clear contact paper or laminate.

STRATEGIES FOR USE   Up to six children can play number bingo at one time. Each child needs a tagboard card and a handful of red squares. Demonstrate the correct way to throw the die, to count the number of dots on the die, and to place a representative number of squares on the tagboard card. The first child to have all the squares covered ends the game. Older children may find the number die more challenging.

THE NUMBER GARDEN

OBJECTIVES stimulate matching skills
develop number-recognition skills
promote number correspondence
enhance counting skills

THEMES flowers
gardens
spring
plants
counting

SUBJECT AREAS math
science
language arts

MATERIALS 2 pieces of black tagboard, 22″ × 28″
1 piece of red tagboard, 22″ × 28″
1 piece of green tagboard, 22″ × 28″
1 piece of white tagboard, 10″ × 18″
library-book pockets
black felt-tip marker
clear contact paper or laminate
scissors
glue

DIRECTIONS
1. Trace and cut out flowerpots from the black tagboard sheets.
2. Cut out and glue white dots on the flowerpots for each number from 1–10.
3. Cut out flowers from the red tagboard with a corresponding number of petals to match the dots on each flowerpot, and glue on a white center as illustrated in the photo.
4. Write the number of petals and dots on the white center of the flower.
5. Trace and cut out green tagboard stems and leaves for each flower and glue the flower to the stem.
6. Cover the flowers and flowerpots with clear contact paper or laminate.
7. Glue library pockets onto the back of each flowerpot.

STRATEGIES FOR USE This activity can be used with a single child or with a small group of children. The objective is to match the petals or the number to the corresponding number of dots on the flowerpot. Ask the following questions to motivate the children:
Can you find the flower that goes with this flowerpot?
How many dots are on this flowerpot?
Can you find that number on a flower?
Which flower has the most petals? The least petals?

TACTILE NUMBERS

OBJECTIVES
enhance number recognition
promote tactile discrimination
develop counting skills
foster eye-hand coordination

THEMES
numbers
senses

SUBJECT AREA
math

MATERIALS
beans
10 tagboard cards, 3½″ × 6½″
glue
scraps of material with different textures

DIRECTIONS
1. Trace and cut out numbers from 1–10 from the scraps of material. Each number should be made of a different textured fabric. Then glue each number to the bottom half of a tagboard card.
2. Glue the corresponding number of beans to the top half of each tagboard card.

STRATEGIES FOR USE
Encourage the children to feel the textured number and then count the number of beans on each card. Extend the activity by providing the children with paper, felt-tip marker, fabric scraps, and beans so that they can make their own cards.

SERIATION CHARACTERS

OBJECTIVES   promote size awareness
develop visual skills
enhance sequencing skills

THEMES   families
frogs
animals

SUBJECT AREAS   math
reading readiness

MATERIALS   1 sheet of tagboard, 22" × 28"
felt-tip markers
clear contact paper or laminate
scissors

DIRECTIONS   1. Draw or trace a series of characters of varying sizes on the tagboard (frogs, snowmen, and jack-in-the-boxes are illustrated in the photo).
2. Add details of the characters with felt-tip markers.
3. Cut out the characters and cover them with clear contact paper or laminate.

STRATEGIES FOR USE   Demonstrate to the children how to put the characters in order from smallest to largest. Then encourage each child to repeat the sequence. Extend this activity by providing materials for the children to make their own characters.

SEQUENCE STRIPS

OBJECTIVES promote sequencing skills
enhance visual discrimination
strengthen matching skills
foster eye-hand coordination

THEME colors

SUBJECT AREAS math
reading readiness

MATERIALS 9 wooden tongue depressors
1 piece of black tagboard, 9" × 9"
1 sheet of paper, 7" × 8"
colored felt-tip markers
contact paper or laminate
scissors
glue

DIRECTIONS
1. Leave one tongue depressor full length and cut each succeeding depressor ½" shorter than the previous one.
2. Make a tracing of each stick on the white paper.
3. Color the bottom 2" of each stick blue; then add one color to each succeeding stick. Thus the shortest stick will be all blue; the second shortest stick will be blue and red; the third stick will be blue, red, and yellow; and so on. Keep repeating the pattern of the previous stick and add ½" of a new color.
4. Repeat these color patterns on the tracings of each depressor.
5. Mount the sheet of paper on the black tagboard and cover with clear contact paper or laminate.

STRATEGIES FOR USE The children can match sticks to the tracings on the paper or they may prefer to build their own sequences using just the sticks. As the children work on the sequencing, you can ask the following questions to encourage exploration:
Can you put these sticks in a row?
Which stick is the longest? The shortest?
Which stick has the most colors? The least?

PIAGET SEQUENCING AND REVERSAL

OBJECTIVES encourage problem-solving skills
strengthen matching skills
enhance sequencing skills
foster eye-hand coordination
introduce the concept of reversal

THEMES clothing
seasons

SUBJECT AREAS math
reading readiness

MATERIALS different colored sheets of construction paper
2 pieces of lumber, 1″ × 2″ × 24″
2 pieces of lumber, 1″ × 3″ × 9″
2 pieces of ½″ dowel, 24″ long
paint (optional)
nails
hammer
drill
pencil
felt-tip markers
sandpaper
glue

DIRECTIONS
1. Drill a ½″ diameter hole 6½″ from the top and bottom of both pieces of 24″ wood.
2. Glue the dowels into these holes (see photo).
3. Nail the stand to the center of the 9″ boards (see photo).
4. Sand any rough edges and paint the wood (optional).
5. Fold the pieces of construction paper in half lengthwise.
6. Trace duplicate sets of clothing, such as shirts, skirts, pants, on the construction paper so that the **top** of each piece touches the fold.
7. Cut out the clothing, being careful not to cut the fold.
8. Add any details with felt-tip markers.
9. Cover the cut-out clothing with clear contact paper or laminate.

STRATEGIES FOR USE Encourage the children to hang the paper clothing on the dowels, matching the clothing on the top row with the clothing on the bottom row. After the children have mastered this, place a sequence of clothing on the top dowel. Then encourage the children to reverse the order on the bottom dowel. You can motivate the children with the following questions and directions:
Can you match your row with this one?
How can you tell that the rows are identical?
See if you can start your row with the red dress (or the last piece of clothing).

MILK CARTON SORT

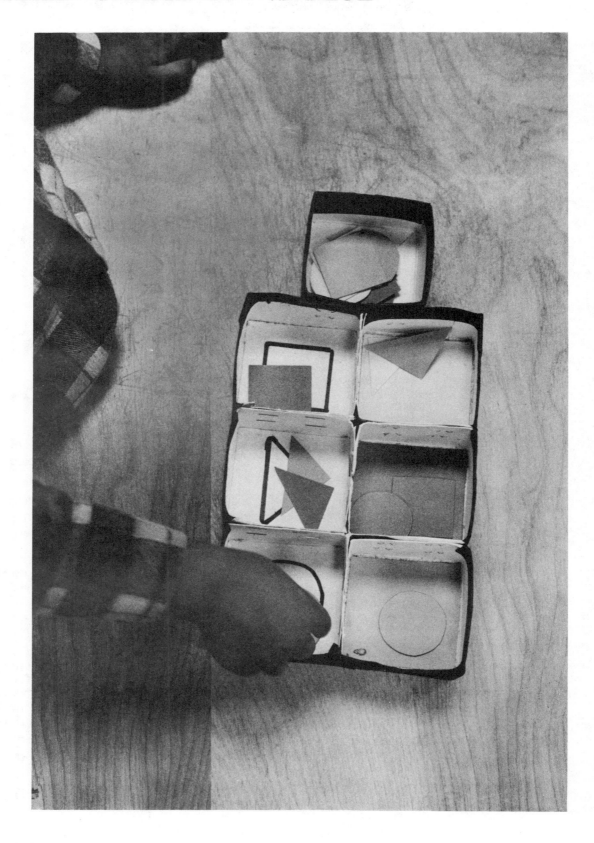

OBJECTIVES
develop color-recognition skills
practice shape-recognition skills
promote visual perception
develop sorting and matching skills
enhance problem-solving skills

THEMES
colors
shapes

SUBJECT AREAS
math
reading readiness

MATERIALS
7 half-pint milk cartons (or equivalent-sized containers)
colored contact paper or construction paper
scraps of red, blue, and yellow tagboard
scissors
glue
stapler

DIRECTIONS
1. Cut off the tops of the seven half-pint milk cartons.
2. Cover the outside of each carton with colored contact paper or construction paper.
3. Glue one piece of red, yellow, or blue paper in the bottom of each of three cartons.
4. Cut out a square, a triangle, and a circle (red, yellow, blue) from the tagboard scraps and glue one in the bottom of each of the next three cartons.
5. Staple the cartons together as shown in the photograph.
6. Cut out matching squares, circles, and triangles from red, blue, and yellow tagboard and store in the seventh carton.

STRATEGIES FOR USE
Encourage the children to sort the pieces of tagboard into the milk carton that contains the same color or shape. To maintain interest during the activity, you can ask the following questions:
Where do you think the blue square should go?
Why did you put it in that box?
In which color carton did you put the most shapes?
In which shape carton did you put the most colors?

TEDDY BEAR COUNTING AND SEQUENCING

OBJECTIVES	foster sequencing skills	promote color-recognition skills
	strengthen visual-association skills	facilitate problem-solving skills
	encourage visual-recognition skills	

THEMES animals
colors

SUBJECT AREA math

MATERIALS 10 tagboard cards, 5″ × 7″
3 tagboard cards, 4″ × 10″
colored felt-tip markers (to match the teddy bear counters)
55 colored teddy bear counters (available at toy or educational supply stores)
clear contact paper or laminate

DIRECTIONS

Counting
1. Number the 5″ × 7″ tagboard cards from 1–10 and draw the corresponding number of circles on each card in different colors.
2. Cover the tagboard cards with clear contact paper or laminate.

Sequencing
1. Draw a sequence of colored circles on the 4″ × 10″ tagboard cards, for example, two red, two blue, two red.
2. Cover the tagboard cards with clear contact paper or laminate.

STRATEGIES FOR USE For counting, the children are to place the correct number of teddy bear counters on each numbered card. For sequencing, they are to complete the color sequence, such as two red, two blue, two red, and then add two blue teddy bear counters. The children can also develop their own color sequence cards.

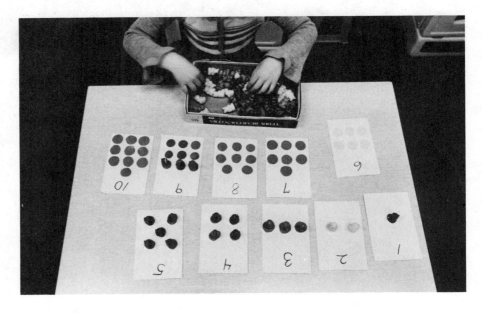

MITTEN
MATCHING

OBJECTIVES   increase visual-discrimination skills
strengthen visual-association skills
promote visual-recognition of words and numbers
practice counting skills
match colors

THEMES   clothing
safety
winter
can be adapted for other themes, such as trucks, fruits, vegetables, animals

SUBJECT AREAS   math
reading readiness

MATERIALS   sheets of red, blue, yellow, and green tagboard
black felt-tip markers
clear contact paper or laminate
scissors

DIRECTIONS
1. Trace and cut out a pair of mittens 5" × 8" from each color of tagboard.
2. On one of the mittens, write a number and then write the word for the number on the back of the mitten.
3. On the other mitten, write the word for the number and draw the corresponding number of dots on the back of the mitten.
4. Cover the mittens with clear contact paper or laminate.

STRATEGIES FOR USE   Encourage the children to match the number of dots to the number, the number of dots to the word, the number to the word, or the word to the word. This activity can be used on the floor, on a table, or by hanging the mittens on a clothesline. You can encourage the children by asking the following questions:
Can you find the mitten with the same number of dots as this number?
Why did you match these two mittens?

GEOBOARD

OBJECTIVES	practice eye-hand coordination
	develop concept of shape
	practice following visual directions
	encourage problem-solving skills

THEMES	shapes
	colors

SUBJECT AREA	math

MATERIALS	1 piece of wood, 11" square, ¾" thick
	100 nails with small heads, ¾"
	ruler
	felt-tip markers
	6 sheets of tagboard, 11" square
	hammer
	rubber bands (colored)
	clear contact paper or laminate
	scissors

DIRECTIONS

1. Mark off a 1" border on the four sides of the 11" square piece of wood.
2. Draw ten lines, 1" apart, horizontally across the piece and then draw ten lines, 1" apart, vertically, to form a grid.
3. Pound one nail in each corner of every square formed by the grid, leaving about ½" of the nail above the surface.
4. Draw the same grid pattern on each tagboard card.
5. On each tagboard grid, draw patterns of lines, shapes, or designs using colored markers that match the rubber bands.
6. Cover the tagboard cards with clear contact paper or laminate.

STRATEGIES FOR USE

The child should be encouraged to produce his or her own patterns first. After this introduction, the child can reproduce the patterns from the tagboard cards on the wooden board using colored rubber bands stretched around the nails.

MUSIC

INSTRUCTION CHART
FOR MUSICAL SHAKERS

OBJECTIVES explore music concepts   practice following directions
              understand symbols   develop eye-hand coordination

THEMES instruments
           sound
           music bands
           music

SUBJECT AREAS music
                  reading readiness

MATERIALS 2 tagboard cards, 12″ × 17″
              colored felt-tip markers
              clear contact paper or laminate
              ¼″ dowel, 8″ long (for each musical instrument)
              empty film containers (enough so that each child can construct one instrument)
              glue
              beans, rice, seeds
              pieces of wood, ¾″ × 1″ × 8″ ⎤
              bottle caps   ⎥ enough for each child to
              washers   ⎦ construct one instrument
              nails
              hammer

DIRECTIONS
1. On one tagboard card, draw pictures illustrating how to make a shaker.
   a. Draw a dowel and a film container.
   b. Draw a dowel punched through the bottom of a film container.
   c. Draw seeds, rice, or beans being put into a film container; then draw a film container with its lid on.
   d. Draw a picture that shows glue being poured around the dowel where it enters the film container; then draw the completed shaker instrument.
2. On the other card, draw the step-by-step directions for another kind of shaker.
   a. Draw a piece of wood, two bottle caps, a washer, and one nail.
   b. Draw a side view of the piece of wood with a bottle cap, a washer, and a bottle cap stacked up on one end of it.
   c. Draw the same picture as in step b, but add a nail above the top bottle cap and a hammer poised above the nail.
   d. Draw a picture of the completed instrument.
3. Cover both direction cards with clear contact paper or laminate.

STRATEGIES FOR USE Gather all the materials necessary to make each instrument. Set up a center where the children can independently make an instrument following the direction cards. The children may also make the instruments a group project.

Once the instruments are finished, the children can play familiar or original songs or explore musical concepts.

INSTRUMENT-CONDUCTING CARDS

OBJECTIVES	promote visual discrimination
	develop eye-hand coordination
	foster group cooperation
	enhance rhythm awareness
	develop left-to-right progression skills
	practice following directions

THEMES	music bands
	instruments
	communication

SUBJECT AREAS	music
	reading readiness

MATERIALS	tagboard
	felt-tip markers
	clear contact paper or laminate

DIRECTIONS

1. Cut 6″ × 9″ tagboard cards.
2. Draw four instruments that you have available on each card (some symbols may be repeated but use at least two different instruments). Example: draw a tambourine, drum, drum, tambourine.
3. Print the name of each instrument below its picture.
4. Cover each tagboard card with clear contact paper or laminate.

STRATEGIES FOR USE

This activity is most successful when used with small groups of children. Either you or a child takes the role of conductor and is responsible for holding up each card. The children play their instruments following the directions on the cards. After the children have learned how to follow the directions, the conductor can suggest how to play the instruments: loudly, quietly, slowly, quickly.

RHYTHM CARDS

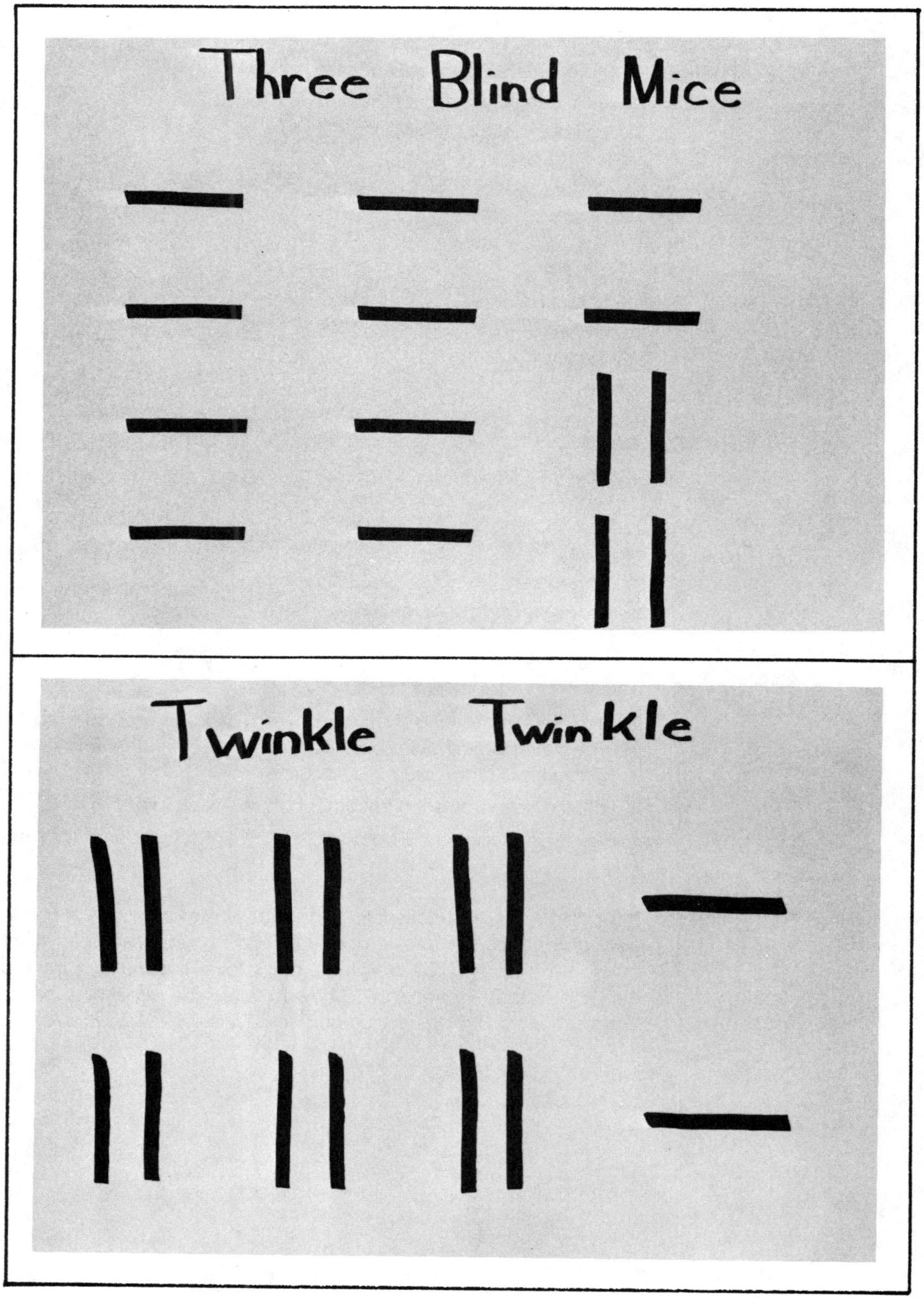

Three Blind Mice

Twinkle Twinkle

152

OBJECTIVES	enhance rhythm awareness
	strengthen visual association
	practice following directions
	develop left-to-right progression skills
	develop problem-solving skills

THEMES	music bands
	sounds
	self-expression
	movement

SUBJECT AREAS	music
	reading readiness

MATERIALS	1 piece of tagboard
	felt-tip markers
	clear contact paper or laminate

DIRECTIONS

1. Choose a tune that is familiar to the children.
2. On the tagboard, draw vertical lines to represent half notes and horizontal lines to represent whole notes.
3. Cover the tagboard with clear contact paper or laminate.

STRATEGIES FOR USE

Demonstrate to the children how to follow the notes, by clapping hands, using the instruments, singing, marching, and so on. Extend this activity by encouraging the children to make their own cards representing their favorite songs.

ACTION RHYTHM CHARTS

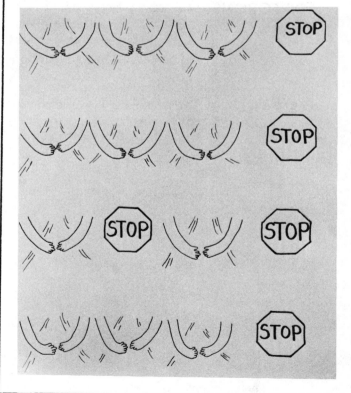

OBJECTIVES promote left-to-right progression skills
encourage rhythm awareness
foster eye-hand coordination
encourage group cooperation
develop symbol-interpretation skills

THEMES rhythm
our bodies
music
self-awareness

SUBJECT AREAS music
reading readiness

MATERIALS 1 piece of tagboard
felt-tip markers
clear contact paper or laminate
ruler

DIRECTIONS
1. Divide the tagboard into horizontal columns.
2. In each column, draw a representation of a rhythmic action, such as patting your head, tapping your knees, clapping your hands, jumping.
3. Cover the tagboard card with clear contact paper or laminate.

STRATEGIES FOR USE Action rhythm cards can be used individually or by small groups. The children look at the card and then follow the directions. When using the cards with small groups, one child is the conductor while the rest of the children are assigned a different action to which they are to respond. Extend this activity by encouraging the children to provide ideas for additional rhythm action cards.

FLANNELBOARD SONG

OBJECTIVES	explore musical concepts
	encourage group cooperation

THEMES	sound
	folk music

SUBJECT AREAS	music
	reading readiness

MATERIALS	felt pieces (various colors and sizes)
	scissors
	felt-tip markers
	a flannelboard

DIRECTIONS

1. Select a song on which to base the felt flannelboard figures. Illustrated is "Hush Little Baby."
2. Using appropriate colors of felt, sketch out the various figures keeping their sizes proportionate. The figures used in the photo are: mocking bird, diamond ring, mirror, goat, bull with cart, dog, and horse with cart.
3. Using felt-tip markers, draw the features of each figure.
4. Cut out the figures.

STRATEGIES FOR USE

The flannelboard song can be used effectively to teach a new song to a large group of children. While singing the song, either you or a child may place the corresponding figure on the flannelboard. Encourage the children to develop their own figures for familiar or original songs.

SONG MASKS

OBJECTIVES stimulate imagination
encourage dramatic play
foster music appreciation
encourage group cooperation

THEMES sounds
animals
nursery rhymes

SUBJECT AREAS music
language arts

MATERIALS paper plates
pink and black construction paper
tongue depressors
glue
scissors

DIRECTIONS
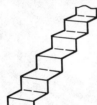
1. Cut holes for eyes in the paper plates.
2. Cut out elephant ears from the pink construction paper and glue them to the back of the plate.
3. Cut out a trunk, 2½" × 18", from the black construction paper and fold it over at 1" intervals.
4. Glue the trunk to the center of the front of the paper plate.
5. Glue a tongue depressor to the bottom of the back of the paper plate (this is the handle).

STRATEGIES FOR USE The children can pretend to be elephants while singing "One Elephant Went Out to Play." You can also make masks for songs about other animals or characters that can be easily portrayed. Appropriate examples include "Old MacDonald" and "Six Little Ducks." The children can make masks to dramatize their favorite songs, too.

PARADE HATS

OBJECTIVES   promote role playing and dramatic play
stimulate imagination
foster group cooperation

THEMES   marching bands
parades

SUBJECT AREAS   music
art

MATERIALS   1 round oatmeal or cornmeal container, 5¼" in diameter
1 large sheet of colored construction paper
glue
scissors
2 brass fasteners
paper stars

DIRECTIONS
1. Wrap the construction paper around the container and glue it.
2. Cut out a round bill with a tab from the construction paper.
3. Glue the edge of the bill to the top of the container and the tab to the inside of the container.
4. Cut one strip of construction paper, 1" × 16", for a chin strap. Attach the strap to the container with the brass fasteners.
5. Decorate the hat with paper stars.

STRATEGIES FOR USE   The children can use the parade hats in individual play or in a small group activity to dramatize marching band members. Extend the activity by encouraging the children to make and decorate their own parade hats for special occasions.

PARADE STREAMERS

OBJECTIVES   promote group cooperation
             stimulate imagination

THEMES   movement
         wind
         self-expression

SUBJECT AREAS   music
                physical activities

MATERIALS   cardboard tubes
            multicolored crepe paper strips
            glue
            scissors

DIRECTIONS   1. Glue one end of a crepe paper strip to the top of a tube.
             2. Wrap the crepe paper around the tube covering it evenly.
             3. Glue the bottom end of crepe paper strip to the bottom of the tube.
             4. Cut crepe paper streamers, approximately 30" long, and glue to one end of the tube. Multicolored streamers are the most attractive to children.

STRATEGIES   Play rhythmic music for the children while they march alone or in large or small
FOR USE   groups. Explore the musical concepts of fast-slow, loud-soft, steady beat-uneven beat, smooth-choppy. The streamers can also be used outdoors. Children enjoy running with the streamers and watching them move.

LIGHT BULB
MARACAS

OBJECTIVES explore sound
encourage group cooperation
foster listening skills
reinforce concepts, such as loud-quiet, fast-slow

THEMES music bands
instruments
sounds

SUBJECT AREA music

MATERIALS bowl
spoon
wallpaper paste
water
newspaper
paint
large, burned-out light bulbs
scissors

DIRECTIONS
1. Mix the wallpaper paste in a bowl according to the directions on the package.
2. Cut the newspaper into 40 strips, 1″ × 4″, and dip them in the paste.
3. Remove the strips from the paste and wrap around the light bulb. Continue wrapping until the bulb is completely covered, including the screw-in metal part.
4. Allow the papier-mâché covered bulb to dry thoroughly and then hit it against a hard surface to break the glass.
5. Paint the maraca.

STRATEGIES FOR USE Maracas can be used by a single child, by a group for a rhythm band, or for exploring musical concepts, such as loud-quiet, fast-slow, even beat-uneven beat. Make an instruction chart (see page 148) so the children can construct their own maracas.

TAMBOURINE

OBJECTIVES   foster listening skills
encourage group cooperation
experience sound
explore concepts of loud-soft, fast-slow

THEMES   instruments
music bands
sounds
self-expression

SUBJECT AREA   music

MATERIALS   1 embroidery hoop, 7" in diameter
18 bottle caps
yarn
enamel paint
nail
hammer

DIRECTIONS
1. Flatten the bottle caps with a hammer.
2. Remove any lining from the inside of each bottle cap.
3. Punch a hole through the middle of each bottle cap with a nail.
4. Paint the embroidery hoop and the bottle caps.
5. Thread about 4" of yarn through a pair of bottle caps and then tie it around the inside ring of the embroidery hoop. Repeat with the remaining eight pairs of bottle caps.
6. Fit the hoop rings together.

STRATEGIES FOR USE   Encourage the children to use the tambourine with other rhythm instruments. They can play rhythmic patterns or explore musical concepts, such as loud-soft, fast-slow.

BELLS

OBJECTIVES   experience different sounds
explore rhythm
develop listening skills
encourage group cooperation

THEMES   music bands
instruments
sounds
communication
bells

SUBJECT AREA   music

MATERIALS   1 dowel, ¾" diameter, 6" long
2 large sleigh bells
2 screw eyes
paint
pliers

DIRECTIONS   1. Paint the dowel whatever color you choose.
2. Attach a screw eye into each end of the dowel.
3. Attach a sleigh bell to each screw eye.
4. Clamp screw eyes closed so the bells are securely fastened.

STRATEGIES FOR USE   Encourage the children to shake the bells in a rhythm band or to the rhythm of a record.

COCONUT CLAPPERS

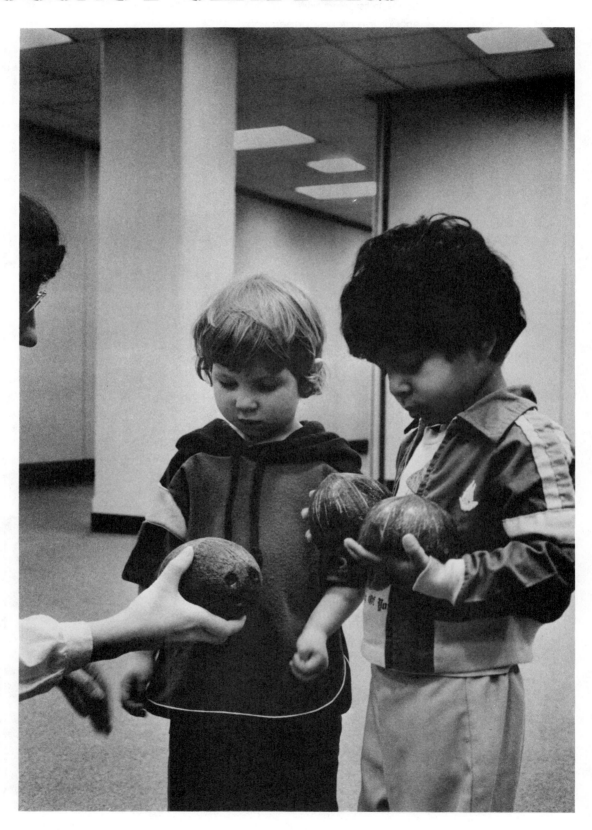

OBJECTIVES   promote eye-hand coordination   experience different sounds
                  explore musical concepts   explore concepts of loud-soft, fast-slow

THEMES   sound   parades
              instruments   food
              music bands   self-expression

SUBJECT AREA   music

MATERIALS   2 coconuts
                 saw
                 knife
                 sandpaper
                 varnish (optional)

DIRECTIONS   1. Saw the coconuts in half and remove the meat and milk.
                  2. Sand the cut edges of the coconut until smooth.
                  3. Varnish the outside of each coconut half (optional).

STRATEGIES FOR USE   Sound is made by holding half of the coconut in each hand and hitting the cut edges of the coconut together. The children can use the clappers to accompany familiar songs, or with rhythm cards or instrument-conducting cards. You can explore the following musical concepts: loud-soft, fast-slow, steady beat-uneven beat, and so on.

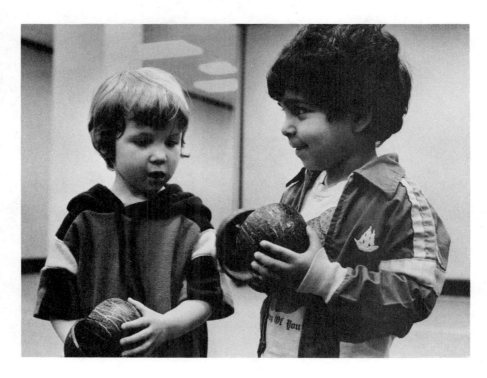

DOWEL BOARD

OBJECTIVES   appreciate music
encourage group cooperation
promote eye-hand coordination
explore musical concepts

THEMES   sound
musical bands
instruments
self-expression

SUBJECT AREA   music

MATERIALS   2 dowels, ½" diameter, 32½" long
1 piece of thin board, 12" long (a paint stirrer works well)

DIRECTIONS
1. Cut each dowel into four equal lengths.
2. Sand the ends of each piece.
3. Glue seven of the dowels to the strip of thin board (see photo).
4. The remaining dowel is used to "play" the other dowels.

STRATEGIES FOR USE   The children can scrape one dowel along the dowel board to accompany other rhythm instruments. Substitute a thimble for the dowel when the dowel board is used like a washboard.

RUBBER BAND BOX

OBJECTIVES
explore musical concepts
encourage group cooperation
strengthen eye-hand coordination

THEMES
music bands
instruments
sound
self-awareness

SUBJECT AREAS
music
language arts

MATERIALS
1 cigar box (or a similar-sized box)
5 rubber bands, several lengths and thicknesses
10 brass fasteners

DIRECTIONS
1. Punch five holes, 1½" apart, in each end of the box.
2. Attach a rubber band to a brass fastener, push through one of the holes, and open the fastener on the inside of the box.
3. Stretch the rubber band tight to the other end of the box and attach it in the same way.
4. Attach the rest of the rubber bands.

STRATEGIES FOR USE
The rubber band box can be held, or placed on a table or on the floor. Encourage the children to pluck the rubber bands with their fingers or strum the bands with their thumbs. They can experiment with high-low sounds, loud-soft sounds, and even-uneven beats.

SOUND BOX

OBJECTIVES encourage group cooperation
develop eye-hand coordination
explore musical concepts

THEMES sounds
music bands
instruments

SUBJECT AREA music

MATERIALS 4 pieces of sandpaper (various grades)
empty aluminum foil box (or similar box)
glue
scissors
1 dowel, ½" diameter, 6" long

DIRECTIONS 1. Glue the top and bottom of the box closed and allow sufficient time for the glue to dry.
2. Cut the sandpaper to fit all sides of the box.
3. Glue the strips of sandpaper to the box.

STRATEGIES FOR USE Use the sound box by rubbing the dowel on the sandpaper. While the children are using the sound boxes, you can introduce such musical concepts as loud-soft, fast-slow, steady beat-uneven beat. The dowels can also be used alone in a rhythm band or in a parade. Extend this activity by having the children make their own sound boxes.

PHYSICAL

ACTIVITIES

BEAN BAG TOSS

OBJECTIVES   foster eye-hand coordination   encourage group cooperation

develop small-muscle skills   facilitate large-muscle skills

THEMES   animals

pets

shapes

SUBJECT AREA   physical education

MATERIALS   1 piece of plywood, 24" × 36"

saw

paint (different colors for each picture)

fabric for bags

filling for bags (beans, popcorn, sand, sawdust, rice)

needle and thread or sewing machine

paintbrush

sandpaper

scissors

DIRECTIONS

Board

1. On the plywood, draw a picture in which you can incorporate something that can be cut out to make a hole, such as the sun, the moon, a ball, a mouth. The size of these holes can vary.
2. Cut out the holes with a saw.
3. Sand all edges of the board.
4. Paint the board.

Bags

1. Cut two pieces of fabric for each bag.
2. Sew the wrong sides of the fabric together, leaving an opening through which you can fill the bag.
3. Turn bag right-side out and fill with beans, rice, sawdust, popcorn, or sand.
4. Sew opening closed.

STRATEGIES FOR USE   Place a strip of masking tape, or mark a chalk line, on the floor to indicate where the child should stand. Then place the board at a certain distance depending on each child's ability. Encourage the children to take turns trying to throw the bags through the holes in the board.

RING TOSS

OBJECTIVES   develop eye-hand coordination
promote visual-perception skills
develop small- and large-muscle coordination
foster group cooperation

THEME   games

SUBJECT AREA   physical activities

MATERIALS   2 blocks of wood, 2″ × 4″ × 6″
2 dowels, ⅝″ diameter, 6″ long
sandpaper
a drill with ⅝″ bit
plastic lids of various sizes
scraps of yarn
paint
glue
scissors
paintbrush

DIRECTIONS   1. Sand the ends of the two dowels.
2. Drill a hole, ½″ deep, in the center of each block of wood.
3. Glue the dowels into these holes.
4. Sand all the edges of the blocks of wood.
5. Paint the blocks (optional).3
6. Cut out the center of the plastic lids leaving only ½″ of the rim.
7. Wrap the plastic rings with yarn and tie the ends of the yarn to prevent unraveling.

STRATEGIES FOR USE   The ring toss can be used by one child or by a group of children. Vary the ring size according to each child's ability. Encourage the children to observe size and number differences by saying:
Toss the smallest ring.
Show me the largest ring.
How many rings are you holding?

POMPON TOSS

OBJECTIVES   develop eye-hand coordination
develop large-muscle coordination
promote group cooperation

THEMES   I'm me, I'm special
games

SUBJECT AREA   physical activities

MATERIALS   2 empty plastic bleach containers or milk cartons with molded handles (1 gallon size)
paper punch
1 piece of heavy cardboard, 7" square
½ skein of yarn (several colors may be used together)
sharp scissors

DIRECTIONS   Scoops
1. Cut off three sides (rounding the corners), and the bottom of the jug to form a scoop. Don't cut off the molded handle.
2. Punch holes, ½" apart, all around the cut edge.
3. Finish the edge by lacing yarn through the holes.

Balls
1. Cut out a circle, 7" diameter, from the piece of cardboard.
2. Cut a hole, 1½" diameter, in the center of this cardboard disc.
3. Loop yarn through the hole and evenly around the disc. Push the yarn together and continue wrapping until the yarn is very dense.
4. Thread a long piece of yarn under and around the inside piece of yarn and hold the ends together.
5. While pulling the length of yarn in step 4, cut the outside rows of yarn.
6. When all the yarn is cut, tie the ends of the threading yarn.
7. Pull the yarn ball out of the disc and trim the edges.

STRATEGIES FOR USE   Encourage the children to work in pairs tossing the yarn ball back and forth. Vary distance the children stand from each other according to their abilities. One child may also toss a pompon in the air and catch it. The size of the yarn balls can be varied according to each child's abilities. Some other suggestions you can make are:
Throw the ball high into the air.
Try throwing the ball close to the floor.
Try throwing the ball to one side.

LOCK BOARD

OBJECTIVES
encourage eye-hand coordination
promote small-muscle skills
develop familiarity with various types of locks
understand cause and effect

THEMES
locks   closures
keys   home
safety

SUBJECT AREA
physical activities

MATERIALS
2 pieces of plywood, 12" × 18"
10 small hinges with screws
4 types of locks: hook, padlock, sliding lock, and bolt
4 pictures from magazines
varnish
paintbrush
screwdriver
saw
sandpaper
pencil

DIRECTIONS
1. Leave one piece of plywood as is. Cut the second piece as shown below. The excess ¼" on the 18" length makes it easier to open the doors.

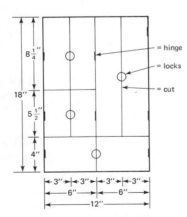

2. Sand and varnish all the wood.
3. Attach the hinges.
4. Attach the locks.
5. Glue pictures from magazines or books behind each of the doors (optional).

STRATEGIES FOR USE
The lock board should be used on an individual basis. You may have to demonstrate to the child how each lock works. New vocabulary words you can discuss are: hook, paddle lock, sliding lock, bolt, key, hinge, snap, metal.

TYING BOARD

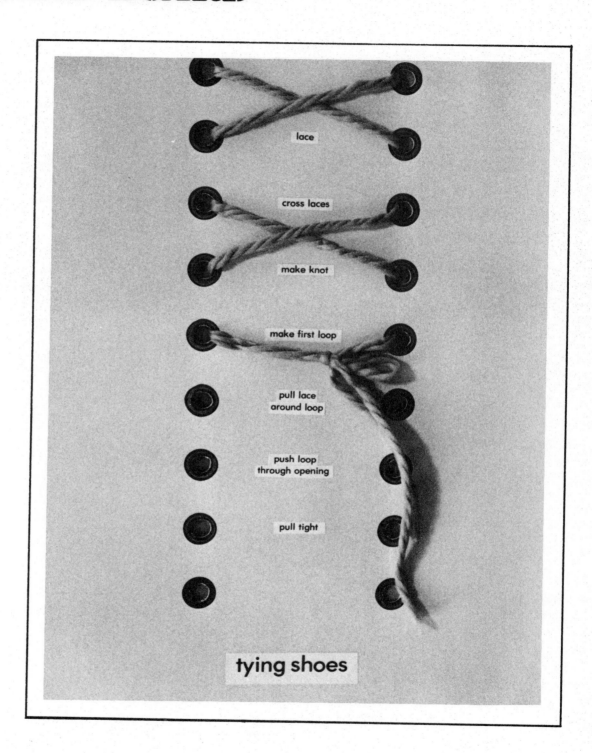

lace

cross laces

make knot

make first loop

pull lace around loop

push loop through opening

pull tight

tying shoes

OBJECTIVES   develop self-help skills
promote eye-hand coordination
enhance small-muscle development
encourage a positive self-image

THEMES   who am I?
clothes

SUBJECT AREA   physical activities

MATERIALS   1 piece of tagboard, 7" × 22"
colored felt-tip markers
yarn or shoestring
clear contact paper or laminate
paper punch
scissors

DIRECTIONS
1. Print the following on the tagboard: lace in a cross, make a knot, make first loop, pull around loop, push loop through opening, pull tight (see photo for arrangement).
2. Cover the tagboard with clear contact paper or laminate.
3. Using the paper punch, make one column of holes down each side of the tagboard.
4. Thread the yarn according to the instructions you wrote on the tagboard.

STRATEGIES FOR USE   You should demonstrate on the tying board first and explain each step as you do it. A child can then use the board independently although you will be available for help or guidance.

SELF-HELP BOARDS

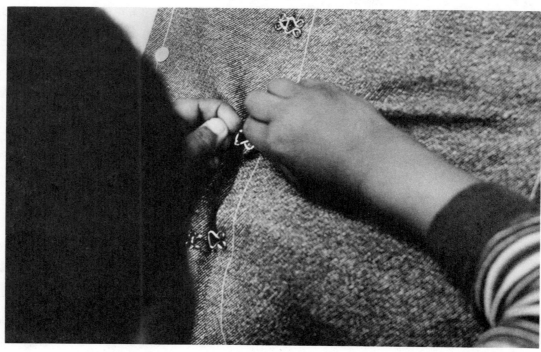

OBJECTIVES develop self-help skills such as buttoning, zipping, tying, and hooking
foster eye-hand coordination
promote small-muscle control
increase self-confidence

THEMES clothing   weather
I'm me, I'm special   seasons

SUBJECT AREA physical activities

MATERIALS 4 plywood boards, 12" × 14" each
sandpaper
varnish and paintbrush
pieces of heavy fabric such as corduroy, denim, canvas
7" zipper with pull
4 large buttons
3 very large hooks and eyes
grommets and grommet pliers
sewing machine and thread
shoelaces
finishing or upholstery tacks
hammer
iron

DIRECTIONS
1. Sand the edges of each piece of plywood until smooth and varnish all the pieces.
2. Cut out and sew a set of heavy cloth flaps, 7½" × 13", for each board as illustrated in the photo. The flaps should overlap.
3. Sew three sides of each flap, turn inside out, and press.
4. On the first set of flaps, sew four buttonholes on one flap and attach the four large buttons to the other flap.
5. On the second set of flaps, attach the grommets and lace the shoelaces through them.
6. Attach the zipper to the third set of flaps. Fold one flap so that it meets the other and pin in the zipper. Then sew it in with a sewing machine rather than hand sewing since the zipper will be used a lot.
7. On the fourth set of flaps, sew the hooks on one flap and the eyes on the other flap.
8. Lay the flaps over the individual boards. Turn under the cut edges of each to avoid fraying. Then nail down the material on the right and left edges of the board with finishing or upholstery tacks.

STRATEGIES FOR USE The children can use the boards to practice tying, zipping, buttoning, and hooking.

SHAPE PEGBOARD

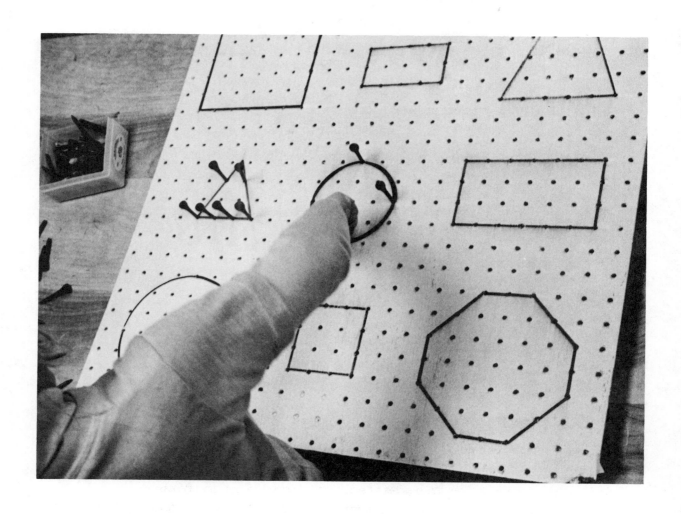

OBJECTIVES   encourage eye-hand coordination
develop small-muscle coordination
understand concept of color, shape, sequencing, and patterning
practice left-to-right progression

THEMES   numbers
shapes
colors

SUBJECT AREAS   math
reading readiness

MATERIALS   1 piece of ¼" pegboard, 24" square, for each board
paint
4 empty thread spools
colored golf tees
permanent color felt-tip markers
glue
paintbrush

DIRECTIONS
1. Paint pegboard one color.
2. Using the felt-tip markers, draw geometric shapes on the painted pegboard.
3. Glue an empty spool at each corner of the back of the pegboard so that, when horizontal, the board will be raised off the table's surface.

STRATEGIES FOR USE   The children can use the board to practice left-to-right progression skills by forming linear patterns with the golf tees. The children can also use the golf tees to trace outlines, fill in shapes, or make their own designs.

BALANCE BEAM

OBJECTIVES   strengthen sense of balance
develop coordination
practice following directions

THEMES   I'm me, I'm special
our bodies

SUBJECT AREA   physical activities

MATERIALS   1 piece of wood, 2″ × 4″ × 5′
2 pieces of wood, 2″ × 4″ × 16″
paint
nails
hammer
sandpaper

DIRECTIONS   1. Sand the cut edges of the wood.
2. Paint the wood.
3. Nail the 16″ pieces of wood 3″ in from each end of the 5′ piece of wood.

STRATEGIES FOR USE   Place the balance beam on the floor, a sidewalk, or the grass. The children can practice by themselves, respond to your directions, or play follow the leader. Encourage the children to use the board in various ways: crawling on it, balancing on one foot, walking on tiptoes, and walking backward.

BALANCE STRIP

OBJECTIVES	develop sense of balance
	develop coordination
	practice following directions
THEMES	games
	touch
	movement
	our bodies
	I'm me, I'm special
SUBJECT AREAS	physical activities
	reading readiness
MATERIALS	carpet scraps or other stiff material flexible enough to roll up for storage
	heavy-duty scissors
DIRECTION	1. Cut carpet so it is 6' long and 5" wide.
STRATEGIES FOR USE	Roll the balance strip out on the floor, a sidewalk, or the grass. Then encourage the children to walk the length of the strip without stepping off it. After the children have mastered walking the length of the strip, encourage them to walk backwards, walk heel-to-toe, hop, run, leap, do somersaults, crawl, and walk on tiptoes.

TIN CAN STILTS

OBJECTIVES   strengthen sense of balance
develop large-muscle coordination
develop sense of rhythm

THEMES   games
movement
our bodies

SUBJECT AREA   physical activities

MATERIALS   matching pairs of large tin cans (2–3 pound coffee cans)
rope
hammer
large nail
contact paper or paint to cover cans (optional)
masking tape or plastic covers to cover the bottom edge of cans (optional)
scissors

DIRECTIONS   1. File down any rough edges on the cans to prevent injury.
2. Paint the cans or cover their sides with contact paper (optional).
3. Punch two holes opposite each other at the top edge of each can.
4. Loop the rope through the hole (the length depends on the size of each child). Knot each end of the rope inside the can.
5. Cover the rims of the cans with plastic lids or with masking tape.

STRATEGIES FOR USE   Demonstrate how to stand on the cans and how to use the ropes. It's important for the children to understand that by pulling on the ropes they lift the cans keeping them in contact with their feet. When some of the children become proficient using the large cans, use a variety of can sizes to add interest and challenge the children's physical skills.

JUMPING HURDLE

OBJECTIVES   develop large-muscle coordination
             strengthen self-image
             promote problem-solving skills
             develop body awareness

THEMES   games
             me
             sports
             my body

SUBJECT AREA   physical activities

MATERIALS   2 pieces of wood, 2" × 4" × 39"
             4 pieces of wood, 2" × 4" × 16"
             1 dowel, ½" diameter, 5' long
             1 dowel, ½" diameter, 4' long
             sandpaper
             drill (electric or hand)
             paint or varnish
             nails

DIRECTIONS   1. Drill a ½" diameter hole every 2" along the length of both pieces of 39" wood
                (don't drill through the wood).
             2. Notch two of the 16" pieces of wood 1" × 4". Glue the pieces together at the
                notch. Repeat for the other two pieces.

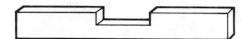

             3. Glue and nail the 39" pieces of wood to the center of the crossed bases.
             4. Cut the 4' dowel into 2" pegs for a total of 24 pegs. Notch the pegs to support
                the dowel crossbar.
             5. Use the 5' dowel for the crossbar.

STRATEGIES   Place the crossbar on the lowest peg and encourage each child to jump over
FOR USE   the bar. Gradually raise the crossbar until each child is jumping at his or her
             maximum height. You can also encourage the children to crawl under the bar
             at its lowest level or to throw a ball over or under the crossbar.

SEWING CARDS

OBJECTIVES   promote small-muscle coordination
encourage self-help skills
increase self-confidence
foster eye-hand coordination

THEMES   home
hobbies
Thanksgiving

SUBJECT AREA   physical activities

MATERIALS   heavy, transparent acetate sheets
yarn, shoelaces, or ribbon
permanent, colored felt-tip markers
paper punch
scissors

DIRECTIONS
1. Using the felt-tip markers, trace patterns from coloring books or create original designs on the acetate sheets.
2. Cut out the shapes with scissors.
3. Add color and details with felt-tip markers.
4. Punch holes around the edge of each sewing card.
5. Cut pieces of yarn, shoelaces, or ribbon long enough to sew around each card.
6. Tie a piece of yarn, shoelace, or ribbon at the bottom left-hand side of each sewing card.

STRATEGIES FOR USE   Show the children how to sew the cards. Then encourage each of the children to sew one or more cards. Extend this activity by encouraging the children to design their own cards.

MAGNET MAZE

OBJECTIVES   develop eye-hand coordination
practice tracing skills
explore magnetic poles: positive and negative

THEMES   magnets
games

SUBJECT AREAS   physical activities
science
language arts

MATERIALS   1 piece of wood, 1" × 3" × 6"
2 ice-cream sticks
1 tagboard card, 10" square
black felt-tip marker
clear contact paper or laminate
2 magnets, 1" square
sandpaper
scissors
glue
paint or varnish
paintbrush

DIRECTIONS

1. Draw a path on each side of the tagboard card with the marker as illustrated in the photo.
2. Cover the tagboard card with clear contact paper or laminate.
3. Sand the edges of the piece of wood.
4. Glue two ice-cream sticks on the narrow edge of the piece of wood about ¼" apart. (The tagboard card will rest between these sticks.)
5. Paint or varnish the piece of wood.

STRATEGIES FOR USE

Place the magnets on both sides of the tagboard card at the beginning of each path (they will stick to each other through the card). Place the card between the ice-cream sticks. The child holds one magnet on the back of the card and moves the other magnet through the maze on the front side of the card. You can introduce the concepts of attraction and repulsion.

FISHING

OBJECTIVES promote eye-hand coordination
explore the attraction of magnets
develop an understanding of color, size, and shape

THEMES fish
shapes
colors
magnets

SUBJECT AREAS physical activities
language arts
reading readiness
math

MATERIALS sheets of tagboard in assorted colors
scissors
paper clips
clear contact paper or laminate
1 dowel, ⅜" diameter, 24" long
string
bar magnets

DIRECTIONS
1. Cut the tagboard into fish shapes and cover them with clear contact paper or laminate.
2. Attach a paper clip to the mouth of each fish.
3. Tie a magnet to the end of a 25" long piece of string.
4. Tie the other end of the string to the dowel.

STRATEGIES FOR USE This activity can be used individually or in a small group. Place blue paper or fabric on the floor to designate a pond, a lake, a river, or an ocean. Spread the fish shapes on the floor and use the magnet "fishing" poles to "catch" them. After the children become familiar with the activity, you can extend it by adding other kinds of underwater life such as octopuses, starfish, and sea horses.

SAND-DRAWING BOX

OBJECTIVES   develop eye-hand coordination
strengthen small-muscle development
provide tactile, prewriting experiences

THEMES   writing
the alphabet
words
creativity

SUBJECT AREAS   physical activities
reading readiness
language arts
art

MATERIALS   a shallow box with lid, approximately 20″ square, 2–3″ deep
contact paper
scissors
sand
ruler
pencil

DIRECTIONS
1. Cover the box and its lid with contact paper.
2. Pour enough sand in the box to completely cover the bottom to a depth of ¼″.

STRATEGIES FOR USE   The children can use the sand-drawing box to draw pictures or to practice printing the alphabet. A gentle shake will erase drawings or letters so the next child will have a clean surface on which to work.

FROG TOSS

OBJECTIVES   promote eye-hand coordination
strengthen large-muscle development
develop depth perception
practice counting skills

THEMES   frogs
games
balls

SUBJECT AREA   physical activities

MATERIALS   1 piece of plywood, 3' × 4', ⅜" thick
paint
3 plastic foam balls, 3" diameter
1 strip of Velcro 2" × 4"
glue

DIRECTIONS

1. Draw a large frog on the plywood (or any animal or object the children are interested in).
2. Paint the frog and the plywood.
3. Glue the fuzzy Velcro to the frog's eyes.
4. Glue the looped Velcro to the plastic foam balls.

STRATEGIES FOR USE   Place the board at a distance relative to the children's throwing ability. Keep score of the number of times each child succeeds in throwing the foam balls onto the frog's eyes.

READING

READINESS

COLOR CLOCK

OBJECTIVES
promote color recognition
develop visual-discrimination skills
strengthen matching skills

THEMES
colors
shapes

SUBJECT AREAS
reading readiness
language arts

MATERIALS
1 large piece of neutral-colored tagboard
1 piece of black tagboard, 18″ × 24″
1 piece of construction paper in each of the primary (red, yellow, blue) and secondary (orange, green, purple) colors
1 brass fastener
clear contact paper or laminate
scissors
glue

DIRECTIONS
1. Cut out a circle, 15″ diameter, from the neutral-colored tagboard.
2. Cut out twelve circles, 3″ diameter, from the construction paper so that you have two circles for each of the primary and secondary colors.
3. Glue these circles, which represent the numbers on a clock, around the outer edge of the tagboard circle. Alternate the colors.
4. Cover with clear contact paper or laminate.
5. Cut out two clock hands, 5½″ long, from the black tagboard.
6. Cover the clock hands with clear contact paper or laminate.
7. Attach the hands to the center of the color clock with the brass fastener.

STRATEGIES FOR USE
The object of the color clock is to encourage the children to move the clock hands to matching colors. You can also use the clock to test children's color-recognition skills by asking them to move the clock hands to specific colors. The children can also name each color on the clock.

COLOR BALLOON RECOGNITION

OBJECTIVES   promote color recognition
develop eye-hand coordination
encourage small-muscle development
strengthen visual-discrimination skills

THEMES   balloons
colors
spring
pencils, pens, and paper

SUBJECT AREAS   reading readiness
language arts

MATERIALS   1 piece of tagboard, 10″ × 12″
1 piece of white construction paper, 8″ × 10″
colored felt-tip markers
glue
clear contact paper or laminate
crayons
facial tissue or felt scraps

DIRECTIONS
1. On the construction paper, trace or draw four children, each holding a balloon on a string in both hands, but leave a space between the balloon and the string.
2. Color each balloon a different color but coordinate it with the string in each child's hand.
3. Mount the construction paper on the tagboard.
4. Cover the tagboard with clear contact paper or laminate.

STRATEGIES FOR USE   Give each child a box of crayons and facial tissue or felt scrap. The child is to complete each balloon string with a crayon of the same color. Then encourage the child to erase the lines with the facial tissue or felt scrap.

CIRCLE COLOR MATCH-UP

OBJECTIVES
develop visual-discrimination skills
promote matching skills
develop eye-hand coordination
encourage counting

THEMES
shapes
colors
numbers

SUBJECT AREAS
reading readiness
math

MATERIALS
1 sheet of colored tagboard, 8" × 10"
20 tagboard cards, 2" square
colored felt-tip markers
ruler
scissors
clear contact paper or laminate

DIRECTIONS
1. Rule off the large sheet of tagboard into 2" squares.
2. In each 2" square, draw four circles, ¾" diameter.
3. Draw various patterns in different colors in these circles.
4. Draw four circles on each of the tagboard cards and color each one to correspond to the pattern and color of a square on the large piece of tagboard.
5. Cover the large piece of tagboard and all the tagboard cards with clear contact paper or laminate.

STRATEGIES FOR USE
Individually or in small groups, the children should select one card and then place it on top of the matching square on the large card. As the children become accustomed to working with materials, encourage them to name the colors in each circle.

CRAYON MATCH

OBJECTIVES   practice color matching
increase word-recognition skills
develop small-muscle coordination
foster visual-association skills

THEMES   colors
matching

SUBJECT AREAS   reading readiness
math

MATERIALS   6 pieces of white tagboard, 3½" × 15"
6 pieces of black construction paper, 3½" × 10½"
6 pieces of buff tagboard, 3½" × 10½"
colored felt-tip markers
colored construction paper
clear contact paper or laminate
scissors
glue

DIRECTIONS
1. Cut the six pieces of white tagboard to resemble crayons as illustrated in the photo.
2. Color the tip and ½" of the bottom of each crayon a different color: red, yellow, blue, orange, green, purple.
3. Paste black construction paper on each crayon.
4. Cut out the names of each color in the appropriate shade of construction paper and glue the letters to the black construction paper (see photo).
5. Using matching colored markers, letter the names of each color on the buff tagboard card.
6. Cover the cards with clear contact paper or laminate.

STRATEGIES FOR USE   The children can work independently or in small groups matching the words on the cards with the correct crayons.

MATCH THE SHAPES

OBJECTIVES   promote visual discrimination
develop eye-hand coordination
practice matching skills

THEME   shapes

SUBJECT AREAS   reading readiness
math

MATERIALS   1 piece of tagboard, 14″ × 15″
black felt-tip pen
scraps of tagboard in contrasting colors
clear contact paper or laminate
cookie cutters (various shapes)
scissors

DIRECTIONS   1. Trace the outlines of all the cookie cutters on the sheet of tagboard.
2. Trace the outlines of all the cookie cutters on the tagboard scraps and cut them out.
3. Cover all the individual cookie-cutter shapes and the sheet of tagboard with clear contact paper or laminate.

STRATEGIES FOR USE   Individually or in small groups, the children should match each shape to its outline on the board. Expand the activity by letting the children trace the shapes.

SHAPE COMPLETION

OBJECTIVES develop small-muscle coordination
develop eye-hand coordination
strengthen visual-discrimination skills
promote letter, shape, and number recognition

THEMES shapes   numbers
letters

SUBJECT AREA reading readiness

MATERIALS 24 tagboard cards, 2″ × 6″
black felt-tip marker
scissors
clear contact paper or laminate
crayon or grease pencil
facial tissue or felt scraps
ruler

DIRECTIONS
1. With the marker, draw a vertical line across each tagboard card.
2. On the left side of the line, draw a shape, letter, or number.
3. On the right side of the line, draw the same shape, letter, or number but make it incomplete.
4. Cover each card with clear contact paper or laminate.

STRATEGIES FOR USE The children complete the right side of each card using a crayon or a grease pencil. When the figures are completed, the lines can be erased with a facial tissue or a scrap of felt. Extend this activity by encouraging the children to name each shape, letter, or number on a card.

BASIC SHAPES

OBJECTIVES   develop visual-discrimination skills
              promote verbal recognition
              encourage sensory awareness
              learn to associate a shape with its written name
              recognize square, rectangle, circle, triangle

THEMES   shapes
              sizes

SUBJECT AREAS   reading readiness
                 math

MATERIALS   4 carpet scraps or carpet samples
             black felt-tip marker
             knife

DIRECTIONS   1. Using the marker, trace a circle, a triangle, a square, and a rectangle on the
                 back of the carpet.
              2. Cut out the shapes with a knife.
              3. Print the name of each shape on the back of the carpet.

STRATEGIES   The shapes can be used as part of a bulletin board and for concept development
FOR USE   during large-group time. Some children may enjoy tracing each shape onto con-
              struction paper, cutting it out, and labeling it appropriately.

BIG, BIGGER, BIGGEST BOARD

OBJECTIVES   strengthen visual-discrimination skills
strengthen matching skills
develop eye-hand coordination
foster size-discrimination skills

THEMES   clothing
families
shapes
farm animals
zoo animals
insects and spiders
transportation: road, rail, water
houses

SUBJECT AREA   reading readiness

MATERIALS   1 piece of tagboard, 10″ × 12″
scraps of tagboard
colored felt-tip markers
clear contact paper or laminate

DIRECTIONS
1. Draw three different objects in three sizes on the piece of tagboard.
2. Draw the same objects on tagboard scraps and cut out each but in two pieces.
3. Cover all the pieces and the tagboard card with clear contact paper or laminate.

STRATEGIES FOR USE   The children use this learning aid by matching the pieces to the correct object. You can extend this activity by drawing three different sizes of the same object on the tagboard and drawing corresponding cards. Some questions you can ask to encourage exploration might be:
Which _____ is the biggest?
Which _____ is the smallest?
Which _____ is middle sized?
What size is this _____?

POSITION-DISCRIMINATION CARDS

OBJECTIVES   develop visual-discrimination skills
             promote visual-association skills
             develop eye-hand coordination
             strengthen small motor skills

THEMES   letters
             shapes
             alike and different

SUBJECT AREA   reading readiness

MATERIALS   4 tagboard cards, 8″ × 9″
             black felt-tip marker
             clear contact paper or laminate
             crayon
             facial tissue or felt scrap
             ruler

DIRECTIONS   1. Divide each tagboard card horizontally into four sections and draw a vertical
                line, as illustrated in the photo, to form a section on the left side of the card for
                the key figures.
             2. Trace or draw figures on the left-hand side of the card.
             3. To the right of each key figure, draw three different positions of the figure, with
                one matching it exactly.
             4. Circle the correct figure in the first line as a guide for the children.
             5. Cover the card with clear contact paper or laminate.

STRATEGIES   Each child should use one card. The object is to circle the figure that matches
FOR USE   the key figure. After the work is completed, the child should erase the board with
             facial tissue or felt scrap.

ASSOCIATION CARDS

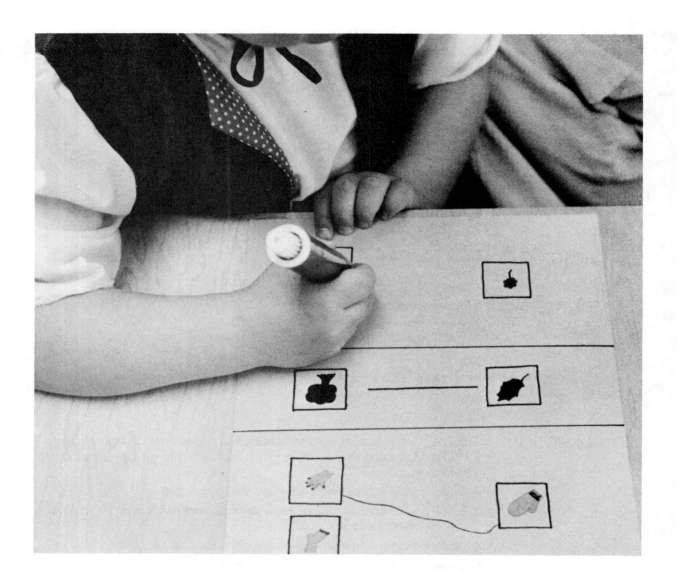

OBJECTIVES
strengthen visual-discrimination skills
promote classification skills
develop association skills
foster eye-hand coordination
develop sequencing skills

THEMES
opposites   clothes
tools   adaptable to any theme

SUBJECT AREAS
reading readiness   math readiness
language arts

MATERIALS
2 tagboard cards, 8″ × 10″
colored felt-tip markers
clear contact paper or laminate
crayon or grease pencil
facial tissue or felt scraps

DIRECTIONS
1. Draw horizontal and vertical lines to divide each tagboard card into four equal sections.
2. At the top of each of the four sections draw two related pictures and a line connecting them.
3. In the space below these pictures draw three pictures—two that are related to the picture above and one that is different.
4. Draw a line between the related objects in the first section as a guide for the children.
5. Cover the cards with clear contact paper or laminate.

STRATEGIES FOR USE
Give each child a crayon or a grease pencil and a facial tissue or felt scrap. The child must decide which two pictures are associated and then draw a line connecting the two related pictures. After completing the task the child can use the tissue or felt scrap to erase the lines.

NAME CARDS

OBJECTIVES develop word-recognition skills
practice printing
strengthen visual-discrimination skills
strengthen small motor skills

THEMES sight   letters
homes   names
I'm me, I'm special   communication

SUBJECT AREAS reading readiness   language arts

MATERIALS 1 piece of tagboard, 6" × 9", for each child
1 piece of ruled paper, 5½" × 8½", for each child
black felt-tip marker
rubber cement
clear contact paper or laminate
water-base markers, crayons, or grease pencils
facial tissue or scraps of felt

DIRECTIONS
1. Center and glue each piece of ruled paper on a piece of tagboard.
2. Print a child's name on the top line of the ruled paper.
3. Using dots, print the child's name on the second line of the paper.
4. Cover the tagboard and the paper with clear contact paper or laminate.

STRATEGIES FOR USE Following the dots, each child traces the letters in his or her name using a water base marker, crayon, or grease pencil. After the children have mastered this, encourage them to print their names on the rest of the ruled paper. Extend this activity by adding the children's addresses. The writing can be erased by rubbing with tissue or felt scrap.

MATCHING STRIP CARDS

OBJECTIVES   develop visual-discrimination skills
practice matching
develop patterning skills
develop color recognition

THEMES   colors
shapes

SUBJECT AREAS   reading readiness
math

MATERIALS   1 piece of tagboard, 8″ × 8″
8 strips of tagboard, 1″ × 8″
ruler
colored felt-tip markers
scissors
clear contact paper or laminate

DIRECTIONS
1. Using the marker, divide the piece of tagboard into 1″ squares.
2. Fill in each square with a different color, but always put the same color in the first row of squares on the left-hand side of the tagboard card (as a guide for the child).
3. Divide the tagboard strips into eight squares.
4. Color the squares on each strip to correspond with one row on the tagboard card.
5. Cover the strips and the card with clear contact paper or laminate.

STRATEGIES FOR USE   The object of this activity is for the children to match the individual strips of colored tagboard with the companion rows on the tagboard card. Each strip should be placed directly on top of its matching row. After the children have completed matching all of the strips, they should try to identify the colors.

MATCHING BLOCK

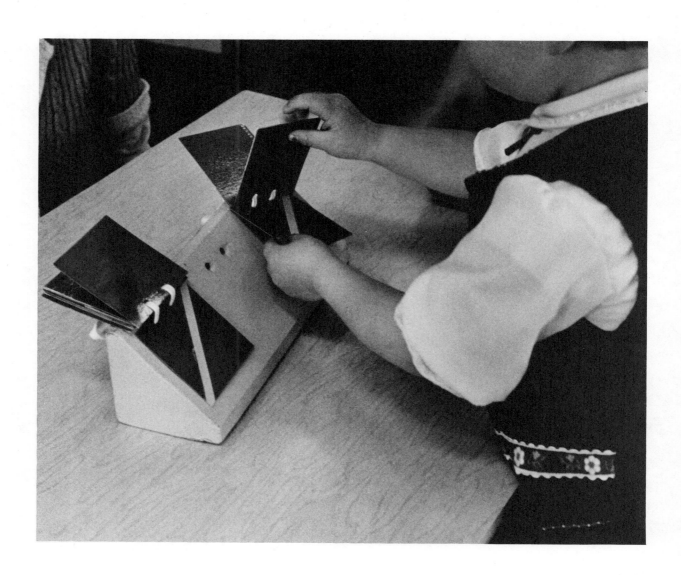

OBJECTIVES develop visual-discrimination skills
strengthen matching skills
practice small-muscle coordination

THEMES shapes
colors

SUBJECT AREAS reading readiness
math

MATERIALS 1 block of wood, 4" × 4" × 11", cut diagonally in half
sandpaper
paint
14 colored tagboard cards, 3" square
drill
paper punch
shoelace, yarn, or string
clear contact paper or laminate
scissors

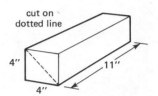

cut on dotted line

4" 11" 4"

DIRECTIONS
1. Sand the rough edges of the block of wood and paint it.
2. Drill two sets of holes in the wood block, 1" apart, 1½" from each end.
3. Draw pairs of patterns on the tagboard cards, such as lines, shapes, or dots and cover the cards with clear contact paper or laminate.
4. Punch holes at the top corners of each card.
5. Separate the cards into two piles making sure that no paired cards are in the same pile.
6. Put shoelace, yarn, or string through each set of cards, through the holes in the wood block, and then tie the strings securely.

STRATEGIES FOR USE The child takes the block and pages through the two groups of cards to find those that match. You can extend the activity by making other cards that relate to a theme, such as letters, numbers, animals, or people.

STICKER LOTTO

OBJECTIVES   develop visual-discrimination skills
practice eye-hand coordination
foster group cooperation

THEMES   animals   zoo
colors   farm

SUBJECT AREAS   reading readiness
language arts

MATERIALS   4 pieces of tagboard, 8″ × 8″
36 tagboard cards, 2½″ × 4″
colored felt-tip markers
clear contact paper or laminate
scissors
stickers of flowers, houses, dinosaurs, comic characters, and so on (available from variety and stationery stores)
ruler

DIRECTIONS   1. Divide each tagboard card in half horizontally and in thirds vertically to create six spaces of equal size.
2. Paste a sticker in each space on the game boards and on each card.
3. Cover all pieces with clear contact paper or laminate.

STRATEGIES FOR USE   This activity should be used with groups of four children. Give each child a game board. The children take turns drawing one of the small cards and matching it to a figure on their own or someone else's board.

Extend the activity by using the smaller cards to play a concentration game. Place all cards face down. The first child turns over two cards. If these cards match, the child continues turning over cards until no match is made. When this happens, the child turns the cards face down and the next child gets a turn.

UPPER- AND LOWER-CASE LETTER MATCH

OBJECTIVES   strengthen visual-discrimination skills
strengthen association skills
learn the names of the alphabet letters
match upper- and lower-case letters

THEMES   alphabet letters
stories
matching

SUBJECT AREAS   reading readiness
language arts

MATERIALS   4 pieces of tagboard, 10″ × 12″   clear contact paper or laminate
30 tagboard cards, 2″ × 2″   scissors
black felt-tip marker   ruler

DIRECTIONS   1. Using the marker, divide the large pieces of tagboard into 2″ squares. (You will have 30 squares.)
2. Print a different lower-case letter in each square. (Letters may be duplicated.)
3. Print a different upper-case letter on each of the tagboard cards.
4. Cover all of the pieces with clear contact paper or laminate.

STRATEGIES FOR USE   The children select one card at a time and check the large card until they locate the matching lower-case letter. Then they place the card directly on top of its matching letter.

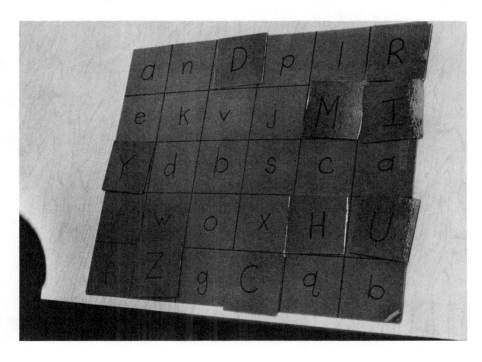

ALPHABET SOUP

OBJECTIVES   learn alphabet letters
strengthen visual-discrimination skills
promote group cooperation

THEMES   alphabet letters
shapes
names

SUBJECT AREAS   reading readiness
language arts

MATERIALS   4 pieces of tagboard, 10″ × 12″
26 tagboard cards, 1″ square
black felt-tip marker
clear contact paper or laminate
scissors
bowl

DIRECTIONS
1. Draw one soup bowl and 26 squares for the alphabet letters on each of the four pieces of tagboard (see photo).
2. Print the letters of the alphabet in the squares in order but leave out some letters.
3. Make sure that different letters are missing on each card.
4. Print a letter of the alphabet on each of the 26 tagboard cards.
5. Make a master soup bowl with all the letters on it for reference (optional).
6. Cover all the pieces with clear contact paper or laminate.

STRATEGIES FOR USE   You or a child draws one of the letter squares out of a bowl and says the letter name to the group. The children look at their boards to see if they have that letter. If the letter doesn't appear on their boards, they should place the card on the correct blank space.

WORD-PICTURE PUZZLE

OBJECTIVES
strengthen word-recognition skills
promote word-picture association
develop small-muscle coordination

THEMES
puzzles
writing
communication

SUBJECT AREAS
reading readiness
language arts

MATERIALS
12 pieces of colored tagboard, 7″ × 9″
pictures of familiar objects cut from magazines or catalogs
black felt-tip marker
rubber cement
clear contact paper or laminate
scissors

DIRECTIONS
1. Glue each magazine picture to the upper half of a piece of tagboard.
2. On the lower half of each tagboard card, print the name of the object in the picture.
3. Cover each card with clear contact paper or laminate.
4. Cut the word and picture on each card apart in a variety of patterns to ensure that the two halves can be easily matched.

STRATEGIES FOR USE
The word-picture puzzles can be used by individual children or by small groups of children. The object is for the children to find the picture and word that match. Depending on their abilities, some children may be able to read the words out loud to you or to the other children.

WORD COMPLETION

OBJECTIVES   develop small-muscle coordination
promote letter-word recognition
develop visual-discrimination skills

THEMES   writing
words
letters
sounds

SUBJECT AREA   reading readiness

MATERIALS   4 pieces of colored tagboard, 6" × 12"
ruler
scissors
felt-tip markers
clear contact paper or laminate
crayons or water-base markers
facial tissue or scraps of felt

DIRECTIONS   1. Draw a vertical line down the center of each tagboard card.
2. Draw horizontal lines, spaced 1" apart, across each card.
3. Print a common three- or four-letter word in the left-hand column. Print the same word in the right-hand column but omit one letter and leave a blank where it should be, such as boy, b_y. Vary the position of the omitted letter on each card to ensure that there will be one letter missing in the beginning, in the middle, or at the end of the words.
4. Cover the cards with clear contact paper or laminate.

STRATEGIES FOR USE   The children add the letter that is missing from the words. After they have used the card, the children can erase the letters by rubbing with a tissue or a felt scrap. You can extend this activity by encouraging the children to name the printed letter, reproduce its sound, and decode the word.

SANDPAPER
LETTERS

OBJECTIVES   match upper- and lower-case letters
develop eye-hand coordination
develop letter-recognition skills
stimulate sense of touch

THEMES   letters
words
sounds
vocabulary
shapes

SUBJECT AREA   reading readiness

MATERIALS   20 pieces of tagboard, 6" × 12"
20 sheets of sandpaper
glue
clear contact paper or laminate
scissors

DIRECTIONS

1. Cover all of the tagboard pieces with clear contact paper or laminate.
2. Cut each of the tagboard pieces in half using a variety of cutting designs: zigzag, wavy, curved.
3. Cut out upper- and lower-case letters of the alphabet from the sandpaper using the shapes in the Appendix.
4. Glue the upper-case letter to one piece of tagboard and the same letter, in lower case, to the matching half of the tagboard.

STRATEGIES FOR USE   This exercise is an appealing group activity. Pass out a letter to each child in the class. Then encourage the children to find a partner with a matching letter. The children will also enjoy matching the letters by themselves.

MAZES

OBJECTIVES
develop eye-hand coordination
strengthen small-muscle coordination
develop visual-perception skills

THEMES
animals
transportation
pets
clothing
insects and spiders
applicable to any

SUBJECT AREA
reading readiness

MATERIALS
1 piece of tagboard, 10" × 12" for each maze
crayons or grease pencils
colored felt-tip markers
clear contact paper or laminate
facial tissue or scraps of felt

DIRECTIONS
1. On each card, draw a symbol or a figure where you want the maze to begin and to end.
2. Then draw parallel lines, ½-1" apart, from one symbol or figure to the other.
3. Cover the card with clear contact paper or laminate.

STRATEGIES FOR USE
The children are to draw a line through the maze from the symbol or figure at the beginning to the one at the end using a crayon or a grease pencil. After they have completed the card, they should erase their work with facial tissue or felt scraps.

SCIENCE

HEARING BOX

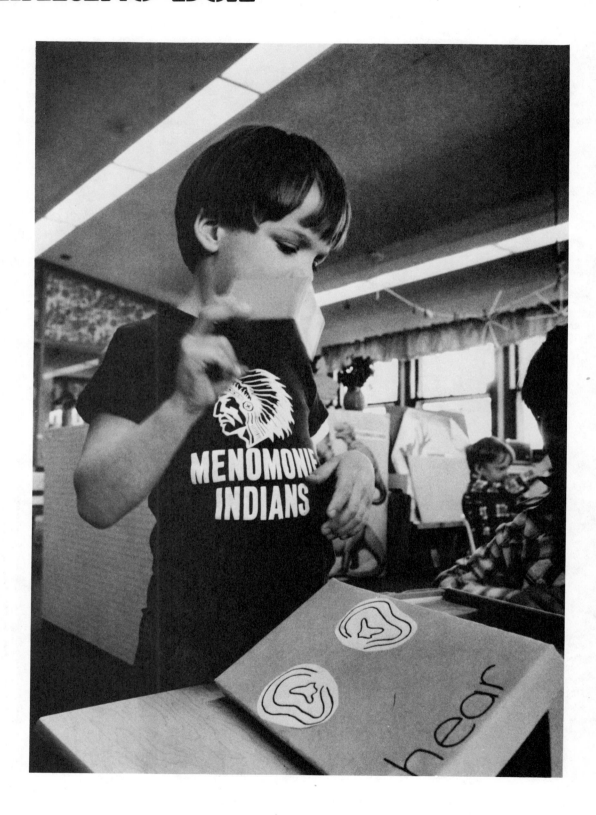

OBJECTIVES   refine listening skills
              foster auditory-association skills
              promote matching skills

THEMES   sound
          senses
          music

SUBJECT AREAS   science
                 music
                 language arts

MATERIALS   1 shoe box
             12 half-pint milk cartons (empty)
             colored contact paper
             beans, seeds, acorns, stones, washers, keys, pennies, nails, bolts, nuts, buttons,
             bottle caps, jar lids, (anything that will make noise when shaken in a box)
             black felt-tip marker
             tape

DIRECTIONS   1. Thoroughly wash and dry the milk cartons.
              2. Place objects for making sound in the milk cartons making sure that the same
                 object is in two cartons.
              3. Tape the flaps of the milk cartons flat.
              4. Cover each carton and the shoe box with the contact paper.
              5. Draw a pair of ears and print the word "hear" on the shoe box cover.
              6. Mark corresponding dots on the bottoms of matching cartons to aid the child
                 in checking his or her response.
              7. Place the milk cartons in the shoe box.

STRATEGIES   Encourage the child to shake the individual boxes, listen to each sound, and then
FOR USE   match the boxes that have similar sounds. Responses can be checked by match-
              ing the dots on the bottom of the cartons. As the children use the boxes, you can
              ask them to search for the loudest sound and the softest sound.

TASTING BOX

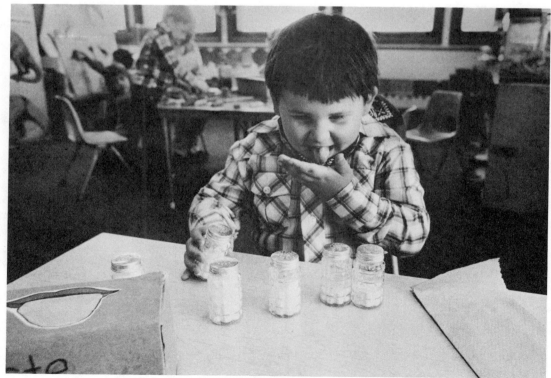

OBJECTIVES   encourage language expression   strengthen matching skills
                 strengthen memory skills   promote recognition skills
                 develop taste discrimination

THEMES   taste   senses
                 food

SUBJECT AREAS   science   nutrition and health
                    language arts

MATERIALS   8 salt shakers
                 box of an appropriate size to hold the shakers
                 colored contact paper or construction paper
                 black felt-tip marker
                 foods that look the same, such as salt, flour, sugar, cornstarch, baking powder, baking soda

DIRECTIONS   1. Fill the salt shakers with the various foods that look the same but taste different.
                 2. Cover the box for the shakers with colored contact or construction paper.
                 3. Draw a tongue and write the word "taste" on the box lid.

STRATEGIES FOR USE   This activity can be used with a single child or with a small group of children. Direct the children to shake out a small amount of food from one container into their hands, taste it, describe the taste, and identify the food. After the children have tasted all the items, you can ask:

Which tastes the sweetest?   Which tastes the most sour?

Which tastes the most bitter?   Which tastes the saltiest?

SMELLING BOX

OBJECTIVES   develop recognition skills
expand memory skills
stimulate the sense of smell

THEMES   smell
senses

SUBJECT AREAS   science
language arts

MATERIALS   6 half-pint milk cartons (empty)
4 large sheets of colored contact paper
1 shoe box
black felt-tip marker
things to smell, such as pepper, cinnamon, dill, perfume, lemon, liquid smoke, vinegar, mint, onion, garlic, yeast
tape
pin

DIRECTIONS

1. Wash and dry the milk cartons.
2. Place each of the things to be smelled in a separate milk carton.
3. Tape the flaps of the milk cartons closed.
4. Cover each milk carton with colored contact paper.
5. Poke several pinholes in the top of each box.
6. Cover the shoe box with colored contact paper.
7. Place all of the cartons in the shoe box.
8. Draw a nose and write the word "smell" on the shoe box lid.

STRATEGIES FOR USE   Encourage the children to smell each carton and then identify what they have smelled. While they are doing this, you can say:

What have you eaten that smells like this?
Find a carton that smells sweet.
Find a carton that smells sour.
What do you think makes that smell?

After the children have completed this task, expand the activity by providing duplicate scents for them to match or provide pictures of each thing that is in a carton and direct the children to match the picture to the scent.

MEMORY-TEXTURE BOX

OBJECTIVES   strengthen memory
develop sense of touch
develop matching skills
strengthen identification skills

THEMES   touch
senses

SUBJECT AREAS   science
reading readiness
language arts

MATERIALS   1 shoe box
1 large sheet of colored contact paper or construction paper
tagboard cards, sand paper, plastic, corrugated cardboard, wood, cotton, foil, plastic foam, pebbles, carpeting, fabric squares, 1½" × 3½"

DIRECTIONS
1. Cover the shoe box with colored contact or construction paper.
2. Cut out 16 tagboard cards, 2" × 4".
3. Glue two cards together for stiffness and durability.
4. Attach the same texture item to two cards.

STRATEGIES FOR USE   The children should describe and then match the textured objects. Extend the activity by blindfolding the children and having them describe what item they are feeling and how it feels. Introduce the concept of opposites by directing the children to find the card with the softest texture, then the roughest texture, the smoothest texture, and so on.

FEELY BOX

OBJECTIVES   stimulate the sense of touch
encourage language development
practice taking turns

THEMES   senses
self-expression

SUBJECT AREAS   science
language arts

MATERIALS   box with a separate lid—illustrated is a box, 6" × 9" × 9"
contact or construction paper
scissors
old sock or mitten
familiar objects, such as marble, sponge, whistle, toy truck, shell, cotton ball, pipe cleaner, toy animal
glue

DIRECTIONS
1. Cover the box and lid with contact or construction paper.
2. Cut a circle, 3½" diameter, in the center of the lid.
3. Cut off the foot of the sock (or thumb and finger section of the mitten) leaving approximately 8" of material.
4. Glue the sock or mitten to the inside of the box lid around the circle opening.
5. Place familiar objects inside the box and put the lid on.

STRATEGIES FOR USE   The child inserts his or her hand through the sock or mitten into the box and picks one item and explores it, guessing what it is. This activity can be extended by the child describing the object to other children, who then try to identify the object from the description.

MAGNET
ATTRACTION CHART

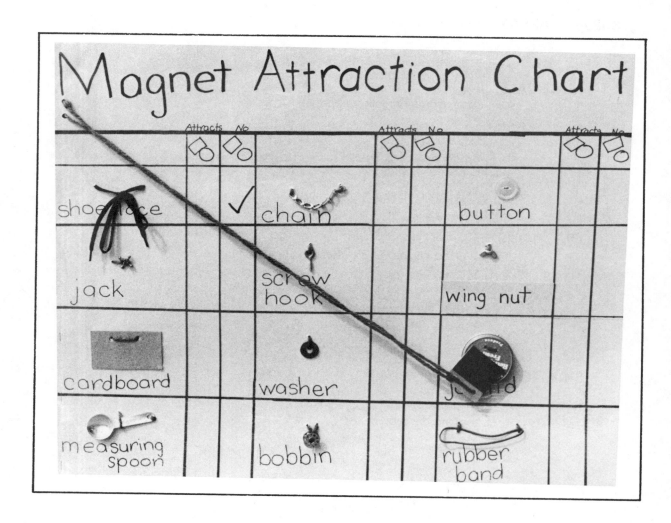

OBJECTIVES   understand magnetic attraction
strengthen small-muscle coordination
foster prediction and classification skills

THEME   magnets

SUBJECT AREAS   science
math
reading readiness

MATERIALS   1 piece of tagboard, 22″ × 28″
magnet
string
paper punch
black felt-tip marker
clear contact paper or laminate
items that will and will not be attracted to a magnet: shoelace, metal jack, cardboard, metal measuring spoon, chair, screw, washer, bobbin, plastic button, wing nut, metal jar lid, and rubberband
crayons
facial tissue or scraps of felt

DIRECTIONS   1. With the marker, draw two vertical lines down the tagboard. Then draw horizontal lines equal to the number of objects to be tested. At the top of the left column, print the word "object"; at the top of the center column, print the word "attracts"; at the top of the right column, print the word "does not attract." Cover the tagboard with contact paper or laminate.

2. Glue one object in each section of the left column and print its name, in lower case letters, underneath it.

3. Attach the magnet to the string and then tie the string to the chart through a hole made with the paper punch.

STRATEGIES FOR USE   This activity can be used by a single child or by a small group of children. The object is to test each item to determine whether it is attracted to the magnet or not and then to put a check mark in the appropriate column. Have the children use a crayon to mark the columns since it can be easily wiped off with a facial tissue or scrap of felt. Expand the activity by having the children guess which objects will be attracted to the magnet before they test them.

MAGNET DOWELS

OBJECTIVES explore magnets
develop eye-hand coordination
develop observation skills

THEMES magnets
opposites

SUBJECT AREA science

MATERIALS 1 wooden board, ¾" × 3" × 6"
3 dowels, 6" long
sandpaper
varnish or paint
paint brush
8 magnets, 1", with holes in their centers
glue
drill
saw

DIRECTIONS
1. Drill three holes in the board to set the dowels in.
2. Glue the dowels in the holes.
3. Paint or varnish the structure.
4. When the structure is thoroughly dry, slip a random number of magnets on each dowel.

STRATEGIES FOR USE Demonstrate the concepts of attraction and repulsion to the children. The magnets will attract if their opposite poles are together and will push away if the same poles are together.

COLOR PADDLES

OBJECTIVES   develop color-recognition skills
experiment with primary and secondary colors
experiment with mixing colors

THEMES   color
sight

SUBJECT AREAS   science
language arts
reading readiness
physical activities

MATERIALS   2 red, 2 blue, and 2 yellow tagboard pieces, each 7″ × 12″
red, blue, and yellow transparent plastic, 6″ × 11″
glue
scissors

DIRECTIONS   1. Sketch and cut out six paddles from the tagboard pieces.
2. Cut the centers out of each paddle, leaving a 1″ edge.
3. Cut 7″ circles from the red, blue, and yellow plastic.
4. Glue each of the plastic circles between two paddles of the same color.

STRATEGIES FOR USE   The children should look through each color paddle first and then see how the color changes by adding a different paddle. They will see how secondary and tertiary colors are formed.

COLOR MIX

OBJECTIVES experiment with matching primary colors
develop eye-hand coordination
promote color recognition
develop small-muscle skills
experiment with mixing secondary colors

THEMES colors
sight

SUBJECT AREAS science
art
reading readiness

MATERIALS

6 baby food jars	food coloring
1 large jar	3 medicine droppers
1 piece of tagboard, 8½" × 11"	tagboard
white paper	clear contact paper or laminate
tape	crayons
colored felt-tip markers	facial tissue or scraps of felt

DIRECTIONS
1. Make color samples using the white paper and the colored markers.
2. Tape the following color samples on the baby food jars: yellow, blue, red, yellow and blue, yellow and red, red and blue.
3. Fill all the baby food jars with water.
4. Put yellow food coloring into the baby food jar marked yellow, blue food coloring into the jar marked blue, and red food coloring into the jar marked red.
5. Put an eye dropper into each of the jars marked with a primary color.
6. Print the words "color mix" at the top of the piece of tagboard.
7. Below this caption make colored circles in these combinations:
   yellow + red =
   red + blue =
   yellow + blue =
8. Cover the tagboard with clear contact paper or laminate.

STRATEGIES FOR USE The children should work with the empty jars marked for the color mix, that is, yellow and blue, yellow and red, red and blue. Using the droppers, they should fill each jar with the appropriate colored water. The secondary color will appear. Encourage the children to predict what new color will result by mixing two primary colors. The children can name each primary color and then each secondary color and identify these colors in the jars. They can also identify objects in the classroom that are the same colors. Use the large jar for the water after the secondary colors have been mixed. Some children enjoy completing the formula on the worksheets. After writing the answer in crayon, it can be rubbed off with tissue or felt scrap.

WHICH MOVES FASTEST? SLOWEST?

OBJECTIVES
promote observation skills
explore motion
develop comparison skills
foster prediction skills

THEMES
movement
water

SUBJECT AREAS
science
language arts

MATERIALS
4 baby food jars with lids (junior size)
4 marbles
clear liquids, such as water, cooking oil, light corn syrup, glycerin (enough to fill one jar)
construction paper
clear contact paper or laminate
black felt-tip pen
rubber cement

DIRECTIONS
1. Fill each of the jars with a different liquid.
2. Place one marble in each jar.
3. Glue the lids to the jars with rubber cement.
4. On the construction paper, print "Which moves fastest? Slowest?"
5. Cover the sign with clear contact paper or laminate.

STRATEGIES FOR USE
This activity can be introduced to small or large groups of children or to a single child. One at a time turn each jar over and encourage the children to observe the movement of the marble. Use the following questions for exploration:
Which marble moves the fastest?
Which marble moves the slowest?
What do you think is inside each jar?
What do you think causes that marble to move so slowly?
What do you think causes that marble to move so quickly?
Extend the activity by having the children prepare their own jars with their choice of liquids.

SINK AND FLOAT CHART

Will it	sink	or float?
leaf		
nail		
brick		
balloon		
rock		

OBJECTIVES   explore the concepts of sink and float
practice classification skills
encourage observation skills

THEMES   water
sink / float

SUBJECT AREAS   science
language arts

MATERIALS   1 piece of tagboard, 10" × 14"
ruler
colored felt-tip markers
pencil
clear contact paper or laminate
items to put in water: a leaf, a rock, a nail, an inflated balloon, a brick
a water table or a deep dish to fill with water
crayon or water-soluble marker

DIRECTIONS
1. Using the ruler, divide the tagboard into three vertical columns.
2. Across the top write "Will it sink or float?"
3. Draw pictures of items listed under materials and write their names next to them.
4. Cover with clear contact paper or laminate.

STRATEGIES FOR USE   In this activity children predict which items will sink and which will float. Place each item in the water and observe what happens. Then check the appropriate place on the chart using a crayon or water-soluble marker so the recordings can be erased later.

WEATHER CHART

snowy

partly cloudy

Today is

sunny

hot

windy

rainy

cl__y

cold

OBJECTIVES strengthen language skills
reinforce the concept of weather
recognize the effects of different weather conditions

THEMES weather
seasons

SUBJECT AREAS science
language arts

MATERIALS 1 piece of tagboard, 18" × 24"
white construction paper
colored felt-tip markers
brass fastener
clear contact paper or laminate
scissors
pictures of different weather conditions cut from magazines

DIRECTIONS 1. Print the word that represents each weather condition on its picture.
2. Glue all the pictures to the piece of tagboard.
3. Cut out a pair of clock hands from the construction paper.
4. Cover the tagboard and the clock hand with clear contact paper or laminate.
5. Attach the clock hands to the center of the chart with the brass fastener.

STRATEGIES FOR USE Introduce this activity by explaining different weather conditions. Then use the chart every day to discuss the weather and point the clock hand to the appropriate picture. To promote discussion, encourage the children to predict when they think spring or fall is coming. Guide the discussion to the types of clothing suitable for each weather condition. Possibly take a field trip to a weather station or a television or radio station to see equipment used by meteorologists.

PLANT SEQUENCE CARDS

OBJECTIVES	explore the life cycle of plants
	learn plant care
	develop visual-discrimination skills
	practice sequencing
THEMES	food
	plants
	spring
	gardening
	hobbies
SUBJECT AREAS	science
	reading readiness
MATERIALS	5 tagboard cards, 3" × 5"
	colored felt-tip markers
	clear contact paper or laminate

DIRECTIONS

1. Draw one sequence stage on each of the cards:
   a. dig hole
   b. drop in seed
   c. cover seed with soil
   d. water seed
   e. seed grows into plant
2. The text can be written on the back of each card or each card can be numbered in the correct order.
3. Cover all the cards with clear contact paper or laminate.

STRATEGIES FOR USE

Explain the cycle of plant life to your class. Then the children can sequence the cards. As they use the cards, you can introduce the following questions:

What grows from seeds?

What do you think would grow from an apple seed? (or an orange seed, a flower seed)

What do seeds need to grow?

SEED-PLANTING CHART

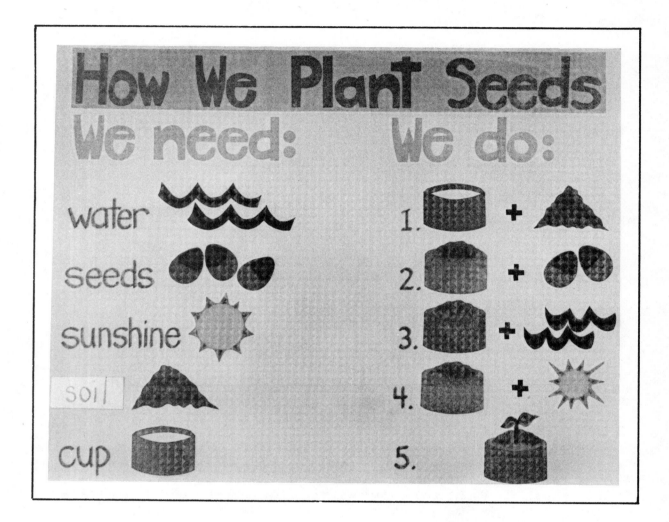

OBJECTIVES develop word-symbol association
follow directions
observe the growth of a plant
practice sequencing

THEMES food
plants
water
sun

SUBJECT AREA science

MATERIALS 1 piece of tagboard, 22" × 28"
colored felt-tip markers
construction paper
glue
clear contact paper or laminate

DIRECTIONS
1. Write across the top of the large piece of tagboard: "How we plant seeds."
2. Below, on the left half of the tagboard, write "We need."
3. On the right half of the tagboard, write "We do."
4. Under "We need" print the words "water," "seeds," "sunshine," "soil," "cup."
5. Under "We do" draw the following steps: a cup filled with soil; a cup and beans; a cup and a watering can; a cup and the sun; a cup with a plant growing in it.
6. Cover the tagboard with clear contact paper or laminate.

STRATEGIES FOR USE Post the plant chart on a wall above a table. Then place the cups, seeds, soil, and water on the table. Encourage the children to follow the directions on how to plant seeds. When the seeds are planted, place the cups in an area of the classroom where they will get the most sunlight.

ANIMAL TRACK CARDS

OBJECTIVES   learn different animal tracks
develop word-picture association
strengthen matching skills

THEMES   animals
winter (tracks in snow)

SUBJECT AREA   language arts

MATERIALS   2 pieces of tagboard, 7″ × 11″ (for large animals)
2 pieces of tagboard, 7″ × 7″ (for small animals)
felt-tip markers
scissors
contact paper or laminate

DIRECTIONS
1. At the top of the card draw the outline of an animal.
2. Below that draw the tracks of the animal.
3. At the bottom of the card mark off a ½″ horizontal segment and write the name of the animal in it.
4. Make a duplicate of each card but cut out the sections so that the children can match them to the original card.
5. Cover all the cards and cutouts with clear contact paper or laminate.

STRATEGIES FOR USE   Children can use these cards by themselves or in a small group as a lotto game matching the word cards, track cards, and animal picture cards to the information on the large cards. Instead of outlining the animal, you can use plastic animals or magazine pictures of animals. You can also use this activity with animal track blocks. The children print the blocks and then match the track to the animal.

ANIMAL TRACKS

OBJECTIVES develop association skills
observe difference between animals

THEMES animals
body parts
seasons

SUBJECT AREA social studies

MATERIALS linoleum squares
4 cubes of wood, 1½" square
pictures of animals from magazines
glue
mat knife
sandpaper
pencil

DIRECTIONS
1. Sand the rough edges of the cubes.
2. Draw outlines of the tracks of the animals you have pictures of and cut them out of linoleum squares with a mat knife.
3. Glue the tracks onto blocks of wood.
4. Glue the animal picture to the cube on the opposite side from the animal tracks.

STRATEGIES FOR USE The children can use the animal tracks for block printing on sheets of paper or on a large mural. An extension of this activity is to go outdoors after a snowfall and look for real animal tracks. This activity can also be used effectively with cookie sheets covered with sand, dirt or snow. The children press the track block onto the various surfaces and observe the different impressions.

WORD-PICTURE MATCH

OBJECTIVES   promote word-picture association
explore plant life
expand vocabulary
develop figure-ground discrimination

THEMES   apples
plant life
orchards
gardening

SUBJECT AREAS   science
language arts
reading readiness

MATERIALS   1 piece of tagboard, 14″ × 16″
7 pieces of tagboard, 2″ × 5″
colored felt-tip marking pens
clear contact paper or laminate
scissors

DIRECTIONS   1. Draw an apple tree on the large piece of tagboard; include branches, apples, leaves, roots, ground with grass.
2. Next to the tree draw a leaf and a cross-section of an apple.
3. On each small piece of tagboard draw one part of the apple and the apple tree—roots, tree trunk, leaf, apple, branches, stem, core, seeds—and print the name next to each part.
4. Cover all the tagboard pieces with clear contact paper or laminate.

STRATEGIES FOR USE   This activity can be used with small or large groups of children or with a single child. The children are to match the small cards with the whole tree on the large piece of tagboard. Expand the activity by having the children identify each tree part and describe its contribution to the growth of the fruit. For example, roots take in food and water from the soil. The children can also use the small tagboard pieces as word-picture cards and practice printing. This activity is good preparation or follow-up for a trip to an apple orchard.

SOC

IAL STUDIES

WHERE DO
WE LIVE?

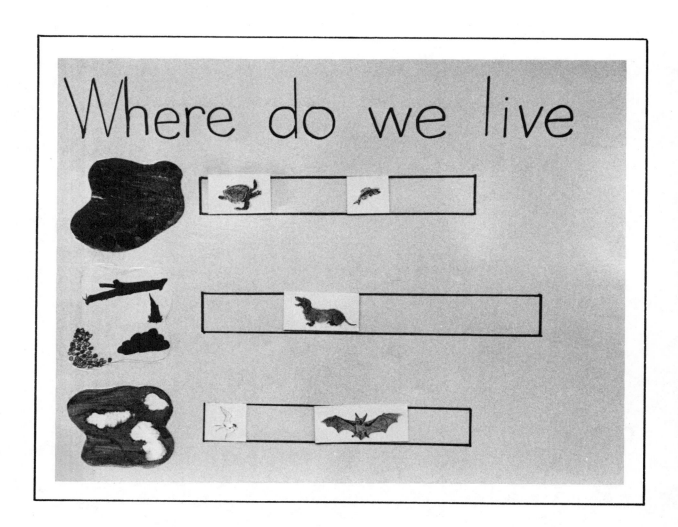

OBJECTIVES identify common birds, fish, insects
associate birds, fish, insects with their habitats
develop left-to-right progression
strengthen classification skills
encourage verbal expression
introduce vocabulary words

THEMES birds   fish
insects   homes

SUBJECT AREAS social studies   math
reading readiness   language arts

MATERIALS 1 piece of tagboard, 22" × 28"
tagboard scraps, 2" square
pictures of birds, insects, fish (stickers, hand-drawn, or from magazines)
colored felt-tip markers
clear contact paper or laminate
glue

DIRECTIONS
1. Glue a picture to each of the 2" square tagboard scraps.
2. Draw a lake, grass, and the sky on the large piece of tagboard. (Or draw them on another piece of paper, cut them out, and then paste onto the tagboard.)
3. Print "Where do we live?" across the top of the tagboard.
4. Cover all the tagboard pieces with clear contact paper or laminate.

STRATEGIES FOR USE You can introduce these materials during group time or to individual children. Encourage the children to sort the picture cards and place each fish, bird, insect card in the proper habitat on the large piece of tagboard.

Introduce some new vocabulary words such as marsh, swamp, nest, gill, feather, and so on.

MAP

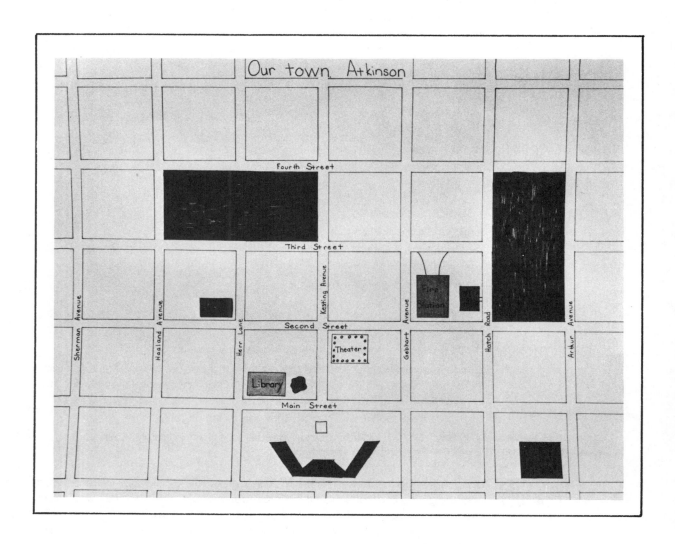

OBJECTIVES encourage exploration of the community
learn how to make a map
enhance self-image

THEMES our community
my home
I'm me, I'm special

SUBJECT AREAS social studies
art

MATERIALS 1 piece of tagboard, 22″ × 28″   yarn or string
colored felt-tip markers   scissors
opaque projector (optional)   map of your city, town, or community
paper   tacks

DIRECTIONS
1. Using an opaque projector, project the city map on the tagboard (or draw the map free hand). Draw the streets and landmarks on the tagboard with felt-tip markers. You may want to limit the map to the neighborhood around the school and indicate landmarks, such as the post office, a park, a grocery store, the school, a church or synagogue, a lake, and so on. Mount the map on the wall or on a bulletin board.
2. Have the children draw pictures of their own houses on manila paper or newsprint and mount the pictures on the map to show where they live.
3. Attach one end of yarn or string to a landmark on the map and the other end to the location of a child's home.

STRATEGIES FOR USE Each child should trace the route from his or her house to the school or another landmark—the yarn should give some guidance. You can extend the activity by having the children help you draw a plan of the school and trace the routes they would use to get to different areas of the building and grounds.

LANDSCAPE CLOTH

OBJECTIVES   learn suitable environments for people, animals, things
promote small-muscle development
encourage group cooperation
promote role playing

THEMES   farm
city
where I live

SUBJECT AREAS   social studies
language arts

MATERIALS   1 square yd of green felt or canvas
assorted sizes and textures of fabric: blue, brown, and gray
sewing machine
thread
scissors
models of vehicles, animals, houses, trees, or "beautiful junk" from which the children can make their own models

DIRECTION   1. Using a zig-zag stitch on the sewing machine, appliqué the assorted pieces of fabric onto the green felt to represent roads, lakes, rivers, fields.

STRATEGIES FOR USE   The children can use the model vehicles, animals, buildings, and so on to create cities, towns, farms, ranches, or their own neighborhoods. After the scenes are created, the children move the people, animals, and vehicles for role playing.

LANDFORMS BOX

OBJECTIVES introduce different landforms and learn their names and formations
translate two-dimensional pictures into three-dimensional models
understand the concept of a model

THEMES water
land
where I live

SUBJECT AREAS social studies
geography

MATERIALS box with a cover (dress-box size)
green construction paper
blue, green, and black felt-tip markers
glue
grain, rice, or sand
1 piece of tagboard
clear contact paper or laminate

DIRECTIONS
1. Cover the box and its lid with the green construction paper.
2. Divide the box lid into eight sections.
3. In each section draw a different land form, such as a peninsula, a cape, a gulf, a bay, a strait, an isthmus, an island, and a lake.
4. Color each drawing to represent the landform and label it.
5. Color the interior bottom of the box blue to represent water.
6. Pour rice, grain, or sand into the box.
7. Make a set of cards out of the tagboard to match the landforms on the box lid.
8. Cover the cards with clear contact paper or laminate.

STRATEGIES FOR USE Introduce the eight different landforms to the children. During the introduction, some teachers prefer to demonstrate each landform by moving the sand, grain, or rice in the box into the appropriate shape. The children can then practice making the different landforms themselves using the tagboard cards or the drawings on the box lid as guides. They can also match the picture cards to the appropriate drawing on the box lid.

LANDFORM BOWLS

OBJECTIVES
introduce different landforms
develop eye-hand coordination
learn the names of different landforms and bodies of water

THEMES
land
water
world
where I live

SUBJECT AREAS
social studies
geography

MATERIALS
6 glass or plastic bowls, medium size
plaster of Paris
green, brown, and blue tempera paint
clear fixative spray
small pitcher

DIRECTIONS
1. Mix the plaster of Paris according to the package directions.
2. Pour some plaster of Paris into each of the six bowls.
3. In each of the bowls, build up a different landform: a peninsula, an island, a cape, a bay, a lake, and a gulf.
4. Let the plaster dry for several days.
5. Paint the water area of each landform blue and the land area green and brown.
6. After the paint has dried, spray the landforms with a clear fixative. Be sure to follow the directions on the can and use in a well-ventilated area.
7. Be sure that the landforms are completely dry before letting the children use them.

STRATEGIES FOR USE
The landform bowls can be used by a small group of children or by an individual child. After explaining each form, encourage the children to pour water into each bowl and tell you what they see.

You can extend the activity by taking field trips to various landforms. This activity can also be tied into the landforms box on page 298.

TRANSPORTATION
CLASSIFICATION

OBJECTIVES   identify methods of transportation
strengthen classification skills
encourage verbal expression
introduce vocabulary words

THEMES   transportation: water, air, land
ways to travel
where I live

SUBJECT AREAS   social studies
language arts
reading readiness

MATERIALS   1 piece of tagboard, 22″ × 28″
½ piece of tagboard, 11″ × 28″
tagboard scraps
colored felt-tip markers
3 envelopes, 9″ × 12″
glue
pictures of different methods of transportation: horse, car, bicycle, airplane, boat, raft, hot-air balloon, motorcycle, blimp, golf cart
tape
clear contact paper or laminate

DIRECTIONS   1. Tape the half sheet of tagboard to the whole sheet of tagboard to create a piece that is 28″ × 33″.
2. Across the top of the tagboard write "Ways we travel."
3. Glue one of the 9″ × 12″ envelopes to each third of the tagboard.
4. On the first envelope, write the word "land" and draw a symbol for land; repeat this process for water and air on the other two envelopes.
5. Paste the pictures listed under Materials on the tagboard scraps.
6. Cover all the pictures with clear contact or laminate.

STRATEGIES FOR USE   This activity can be used either by a small group of children or by a single child. The object is to place each picture into the appropriate envelope: bicycle / land, airplane / air, and so on.

Extend the activity by having the children browse through magazines to find materials that will supplement this classification or to create their own classification charts.

OCCUPATION CLASSIFICATION

OBJECTIVES   develop classification skills
stimulate vocabulary development
help conceptualize occupations

THEMES   community helpers
occupations
family

SUBJECT AREAS   social studies
language arts
math

MATERIALS   2 pieces of tagboard, 10" × 12"
12 pieces of tagboard, 3½" × 4"
felt-tip markers
pictures from magazines
scissors
clear contact paper or laminate

DIRECTIONS

1. On each 10" × 12" card draw a person (either male or female). The person should be dressed in clothes associated with an occupation. (Illustrated are doctor and firefighter.)

2. Write the name of the occupation at the top of each card in lower case letters.

3. On the smaller tagboard cards draw the tools used in each occupation. Items for doctors might include medical bag, stethoscope, thermometer, tongue depressor, bandages. Items for firefighters might include hat, ax, ladder, hose, and firetruck. You can substitute pictures from magazines instead of drawing the objects.

4. Cover all the tagboard cards with clear contact or laminate.

STRATEGIES FOR USE   This activity can be used with a small group of children or with an individual child. Have the children sort the small cards and match them to the appropriate occupation card. As an introduction or during the activity, you can emphasize the names of the tools to expand the children's vocabulary.

TIN CAN PUPPETS

OBJECTIVES promote verbal expression
foster social involvement
encourage creative expression
stimulate dramatic expression

THEMES family   storytelling
puppets   communication
community helper   emotions

SUBJECT AREAS social studies   language arts
children's literature   art

MATERIALS empty tin cans, juice cans
scraps of felt, fabric, aluminum foil, fur, yarn
any other accessories suitable for story characters
felt-tip markers
glue
scissors

DIRECTIONS
1. Cover the cans with felt or fabric.
2. If desired, glue another piece of fabric on top of the felt to make a face.
3. Glue on appropriate pieces of felt or fabric for clothing, such as collar, suspenders, cape.
4. Draw on the facial features with felt-tip markers.
5. Glue yarn pieces for hair around the face and the back of the head.
6. If appropriate, construct a hat out of tagboard and cover it with felt or fabric.

STRATEGIES FOR USE These puppets can be used for discussing families and feelings. Then encourage the children to use the puppets to re-create everyday events. The children can also make their own puppets based on familiar or self-created story characters.

HOUSEHOLD
SORTING
BOX

OBJECTIVES identify common household items   strengthen eye-hand coordination
develop classification skills

THEMES homes   touch
I'm me, I'm special

SUBJECT AREAS social studies
math

MATERIALS 1 large cardboard box with lid
3 small cardboard boxes, all about the same size, with no lids
colored construction paper, contact paper, or wrapping paper
colored felt-tip markers
glue
tape
scissors
household items: plates, cups, cookie cutters, measuring cups, toothbrush, nails, bolts, screws, hammer, hairbrush, scissors, empty lipstick tube, toilet paper, empty adhesive bandage box, telephone, washcloth, towel, heating pad, sponge, sandpaper, teapot, baby bottle, empty shampoo bottle, pieces of wood, dustpan

DIRECTIONS 1. Put all the household items listed under Materials in the large box.
2. Cover the three smaller boxes with colored construction paper, contact paper, or wrapping paper.
3. On the outside of each of these boxes, draw a room from a house, such as a kitchen, a bathroom, and a workshop. The kitchen has a stove, a refrigerator, a sink, and a cupboard. The bathroom has a tub, a sink, a toilet, a towel rack, a toilet-paper holder. The workshop has a table saw, saw horses, tools, and a storage cabinet.
4. Write the name of each room under its picture.

STRATEGIES FOR USE Put the three boxes on the floor. The child takes a household item from the large box and places it in the box that represents the room where the item would commonly be found. For example, washcloths would be placed in the box representing a bathroom. When the child has finished sorting all the items from the large box, check that everything was properly sorted. The child should then return all the items to the large box.

SEASONAL FABRIC SORT

OBJECTIVES
develop classification skills
understand how weather changes relate to the seasons
understand the sequence of seasons
identify the seasons
encourage verbal expression
stimulate sense of touch

THEMES
weather   clothing
seasons

SUBJECT AREAS
social studies   math
language arts

MATERIALS
pictures, cut from magazines or calendars, depicting each of the seasons
construction paper, 7½" × 9"
scissors
clear contact paper or laminate
glue
felt-tip marker
3" squares of fabric

DIRECTIONS
1. Glue each picture to a sheet of construction paper.
2. Write the name of each season below each picture.
3. Cover the construction paper with clear contact or laminate.

STRATEGIES FOR USE
This activity can be used by one child or by a small group of children. Spread the pictures of the seasons on a table or on the floor. The child is to sort the fabric according to the appropriate season and place the fabric on the picture of that season.

Instead of using pieces of fabric, you can use actual clothing, which the child sorts in the same way.

DRESSING DOLL

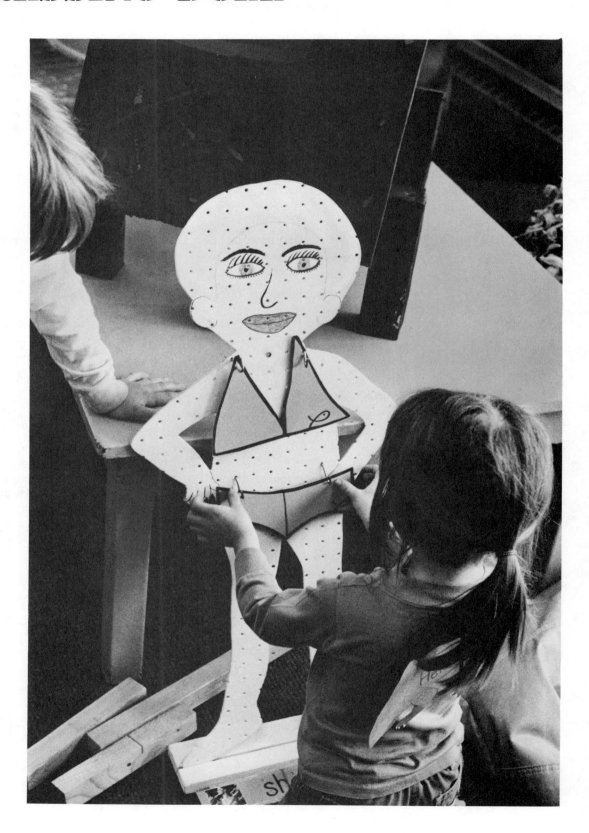

OBJECTIVES   match clothing to the correct parts of the body

develop eye-hand coordination

learn to move in response to verbal directions

differentiate between left and right

learn the names of body parts

give directions to others

THEMES   I'm me, I'm special

clothing

seasons

SUBJECT AREAS   social studies

language arts

reading readiness

physical activities

MATERIALS   jigsaw

flesh-tone paint

paper punch

pegboard hooks

various colors of tagboard

1½ yd of clear plastic laminate or clear contact paper

1 piece of pegboard, 36" square

felt-tip markers

newspapers

DIRECTIONS

1. Trace a human figure on the piece of pegboard and cut it out with the jigsaw.
2. Paint the body and add the facial features with felt-tip markers.
3. Trace the body on newspaper, which will serve as a pattern.
4. Using the pattern, trace a sweater, coat, jacket, dress, pants, and shorts on different pieces of colored tagboard.
5. Cut out and punch holes in all the clothing and label it. Cover with clear contact paper or laminate.

STRATEGIES FOR USE

The children are to dress the doll according to the current weather conditions. (The clothes are hung on the pegboard hooks.) Discuss the names for various body parts and differentiate between the left and right sides of the figure.

Extend the activity by having the children design clothing for the dressing doll. Write the name of each article of clothing on tagboard cards, show the cards to the children, and have them match the word on the card with the word written on the clothing.

ATTENDANCE CHART

OBJECTIVES   promote name recognition
develop group awareness
encourage counting skills

THEME   I'm me, I'm special

SUBJECT AREAS   social studies
reading readiness

MATERIALS   2½ sheets of 22″ × 28″ tagboard
library pockets—one for every child in the class
felt-tip markers
scissors
paper clips
glue
single-edge razor blade
clear contact paper or laminate

DIRECTIONS
1. At the top of one piece of tagboard print "children at school."
2. Under this title, mount the library pockets.
3. Cover the chart with clear contact paper or laminate and slit pockets open with single-edge razor blade.
4. Cut cards, 1½″ × 3½″, from the second piece of tagboard (one for each child in the class).
5. Print the name of each child in the class at the top of a card and cover the cards with clear contact paper or laminate.
6. Attach each of the cards to a library pocket with a paper clip.
7. Make another set of cards with each of the children's names written on them. These should fit into the library pockets but can be a geometric shape, an animal shape, a photograph of the child, and so on.
8. Cover all these cards with laminate or clear contact paper.

STRATEGIES FOR USE   When they arrive at school, each of the children finds his or her own card and then proceeds to place it in the pocket that has his or her name on it. During group time you and the children can check the chart and count how many children are present and how many are absent.

CALENDAR

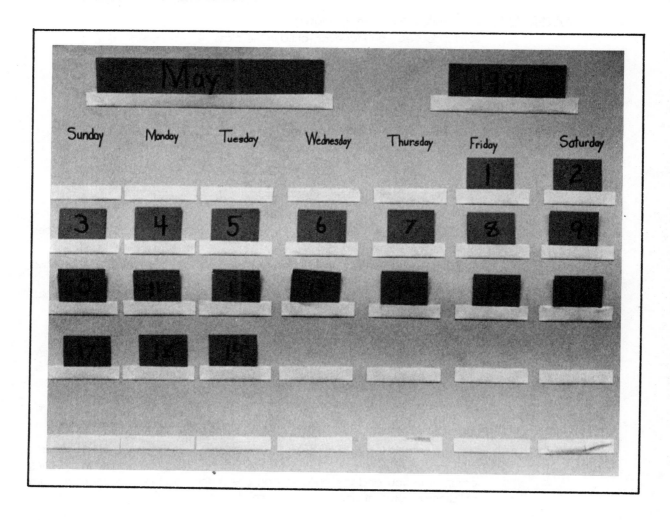

OBJECTIVES   explore the function of a calendar
practice sequencing skills
understand the concept of time

THEMES   time
clocks
numbers
calendars
seasons

SUBJECT AREAS   math
social studies

MATERIALS   2 pieces of tagboard, each 22″ × 28″
felt-tip markers
clear contact paper or laminate
glue or tape
scissors
single-edge razor blade

DIRECTIONS   1. With the felt-tip marker, divide one piece of tagboard into seven vertical sections and seven horizontal sections. (Divisions are for day, date, month, year.)
2. Cut 31 pieces of tagboard, 2″ × 3½″. Fold these pieces in half lengthwise and glue one in each section (see photo).
3. Print the days of the week across the top of the calendar.
4. Cut two pieces of tagboard, 2″ × 12″ and 2″ × 7″, fold in half lengthwise, and glue to the top of the calendar (see photo).
5. Cover the entire calendar with clear contact paper or laminate and slit each pocket open.
6. Cut 31 cards, 2″ square, out of the tagboard and write the numbers 1 through 31, one on each card.
7. Cut 12 tagboard cards, 2″ × 11″ and write the name of each month on a card.
8. Cut a tagboard card, 2″ × 6″, and write the year on it.
9. Cover all the tagboard cards with clear contact paper or laminate.

STRATEGIES FOR USE   This calendar can be used every day to identify the date, day of the week, month, and year. The children can identify special events at school or holidays and use the calendar to count down to the days.

Extend this activity by making cards to represent holidays, birthdays, and special events. Cards with weather symbols can also be made to put into the pockets. At the end of each day, the children can discuss what they enjoyed doing on that particular day. Draw a symbol of the event on a card and place it in the appropriate pocket.

CLOCK

OBJECTIVES   encourage counting skills
facilitate number recognition
practice ordering numbers
learn how to tell time

THEMES   time   numbers
clocks   calendars

SUBJECT AREAS   social studies
math

MATERIALS   2 pieces of tagboard in contrasting colors, 22″ × 28″
brass fastener
felt-tip markers
clear contact paper or laminate

DIRECTIONS
1. Cut a circle 18″ in diameter from one piece of tagboard.
2. Cut a 2″ slot at the position of each hour on the tagboard circle.
3. Cut 12 cards, 2″ × 3⅓″, from the other piece of tagboard.
4. Write a number, 1 through 12, on the upper half of each card.
5. Cut a piece of tagboard, 4″ × 7″, and glue it on the reverse side of the clock face so it can be used as a pocket to hold the numbered cards.
6. Cut out two hands for the clock, making one approximately 2″ longer than the other.
7. Cover all of the tagboard pieces with clear contact paper or laminate.
8. Attach the hands to the face of the clock with a brass fastener.

STRATEGIES FOR USE   This clock is most effective when introduced to small groups of children. After explaining the function of the clock and what each hand represents, encourage the children to set the clock at various times.

The clock may also be used to indicate the time a special event will take place, such as the time a special guest will come to school, the time of a field trip, or the time school is out.

WHAT CAN YOU DO IN THE DARK?

OBJECTIVES   develop visual-association skills
develop memory skills
encourage word-picture association

THEMES   energy conservation
day / night

SUBJECT AREAS   social studies
reading readiness
language arts

MATERIALS   28 black tagboard cards, 3″ × 5″
colored construction paper
glue

DIRECTIONS
1. Using the patterns in the Appendix, cut out duplicates of each picture from colored construction paper and mount on the black tagboard cards.
2. Write captions on construction paper and mount on the tagboard cards. (For captions, see Appendix.)
3. Cover all the cards with clear contact paper or laminate.

STRATEGIES FOR USE   This game is played like concentration. Put the cards face down on the table and have the children select two at a time trying to make a match. When they have a match, the children can read the caption or simply tell how the idea on the card can save energy.

APPENDIX

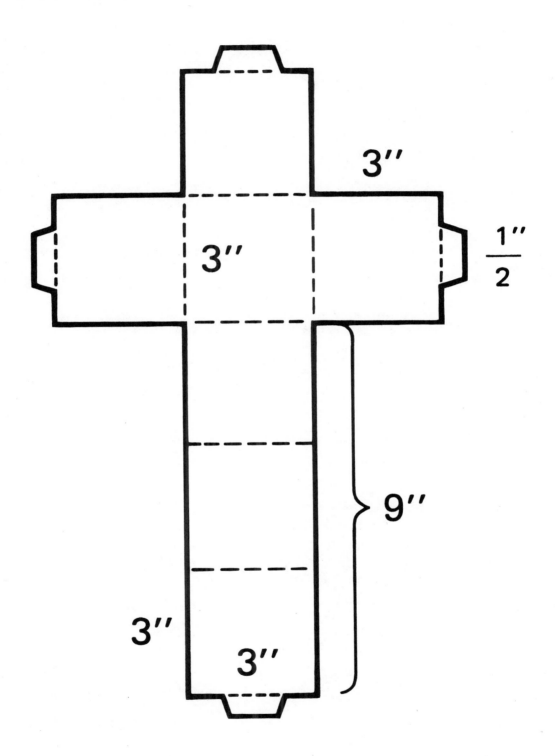

Pattern for Dice Games

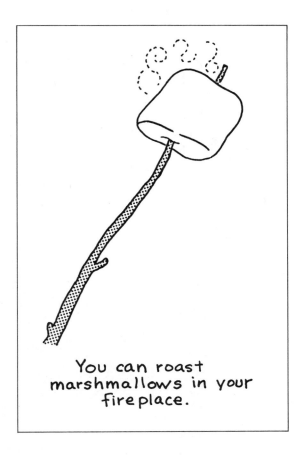

You can roast
marshmallows in your
fireplace.

You can look at
the stars and find
the Big Dipper.

Patterns for "What Can You Do In the Dark?"

You can tell
ghost stories.

You can have
a campfire..

You can light
a candle.

You can sleep
with your
night light off.

You can pretend
that black is your
favorite color.

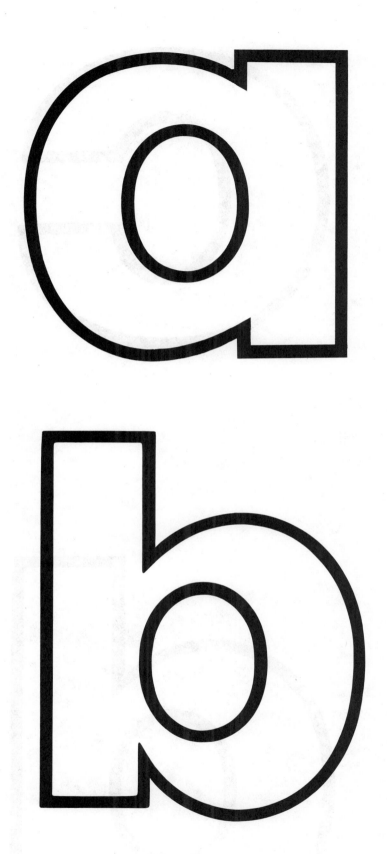

Patterns for Alphabet and Numbers

c

d

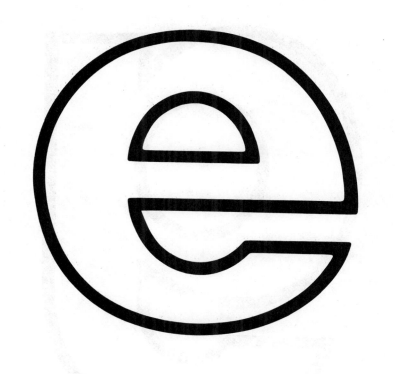

e

f

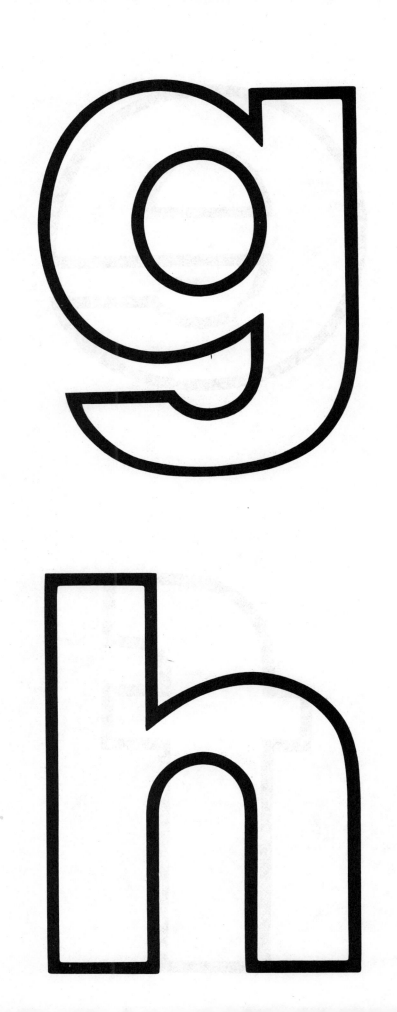

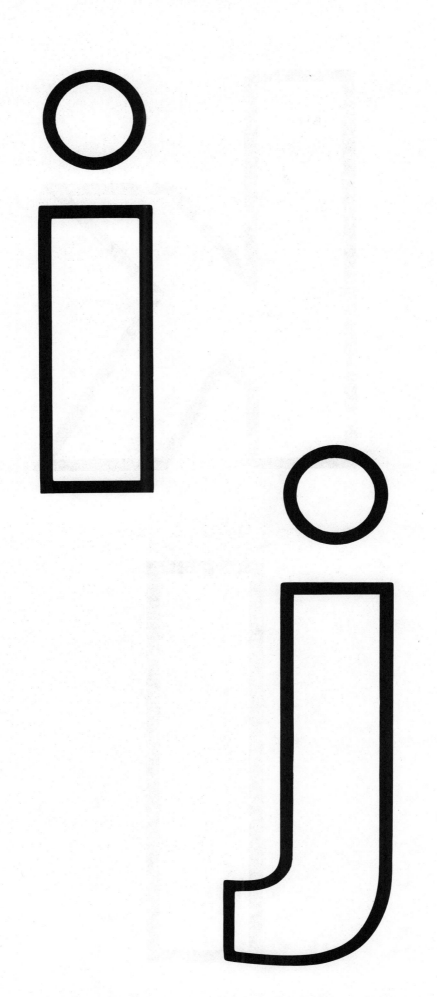

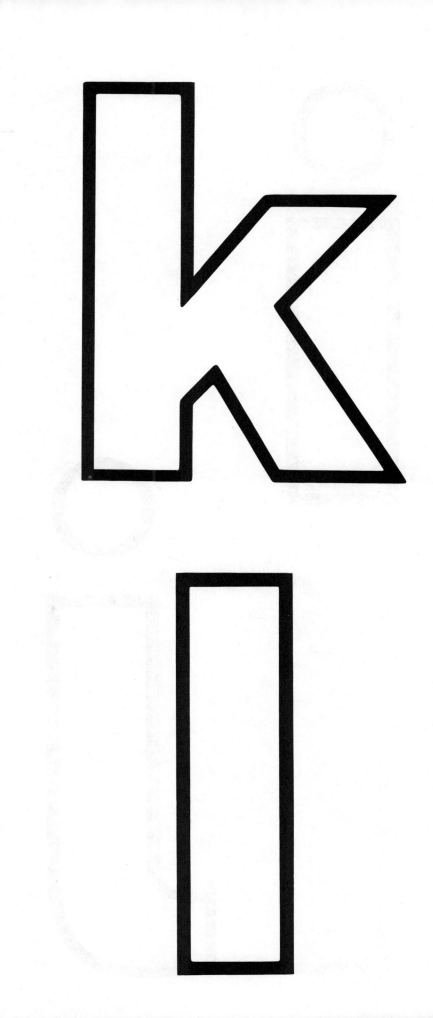

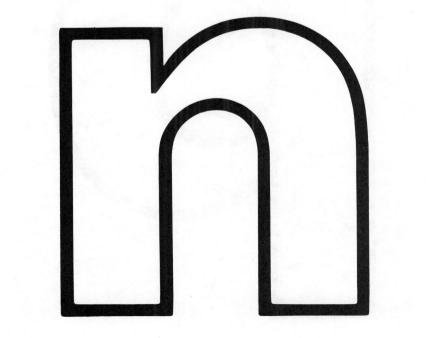

o

p

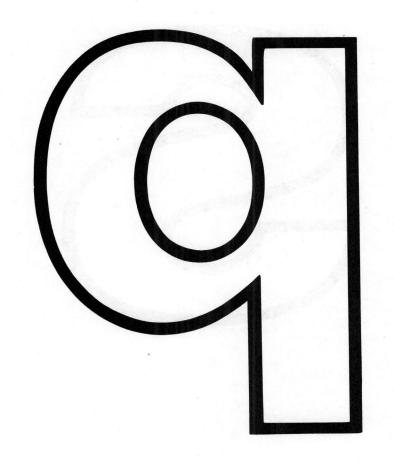

q

r

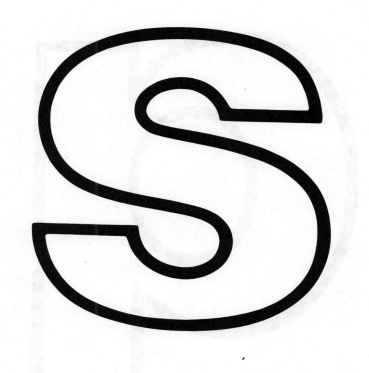

s

t

u

v

W

X

y

z

4

A

B

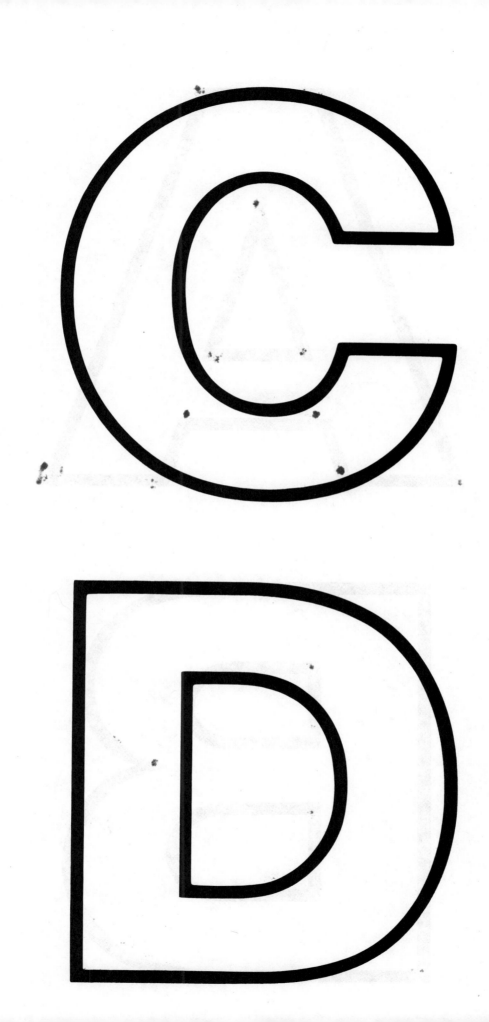

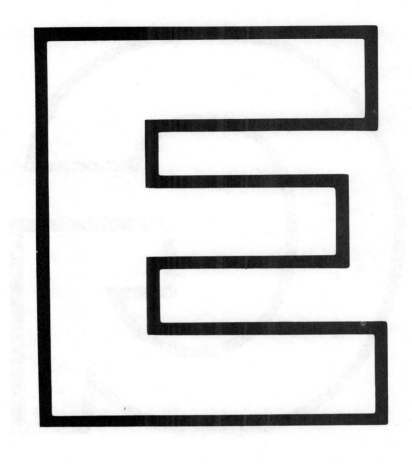

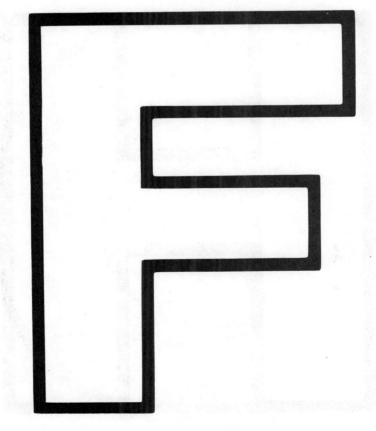

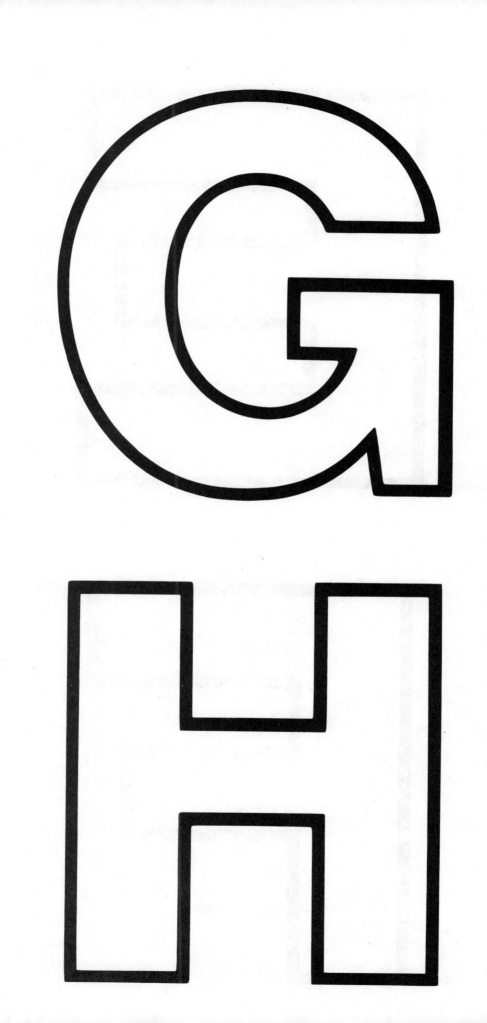

2

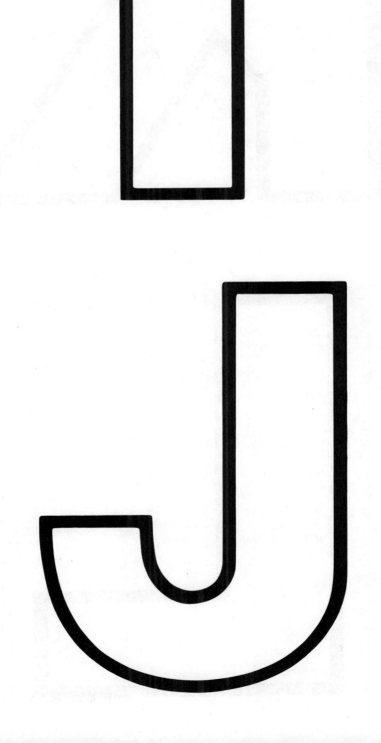

K

L

3

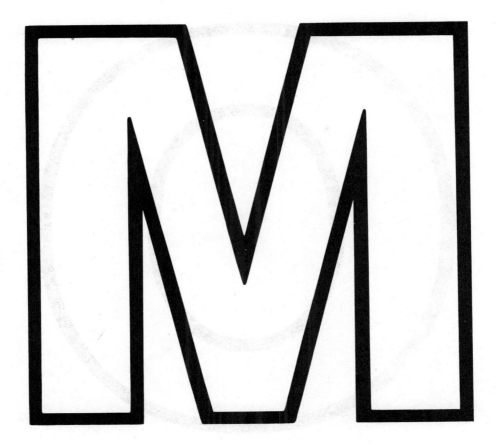

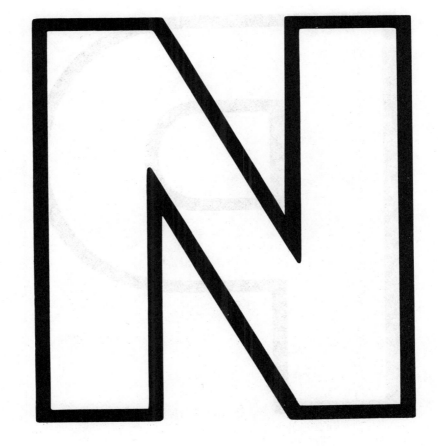

3

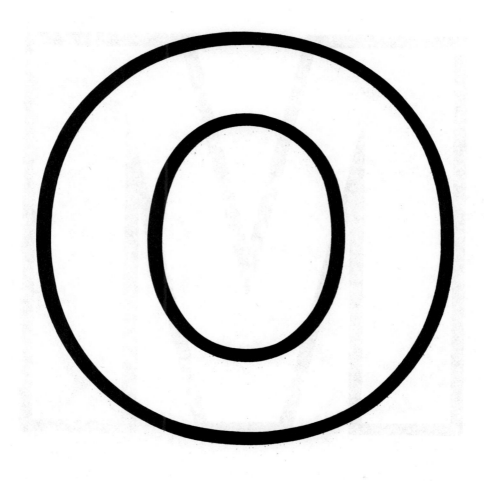

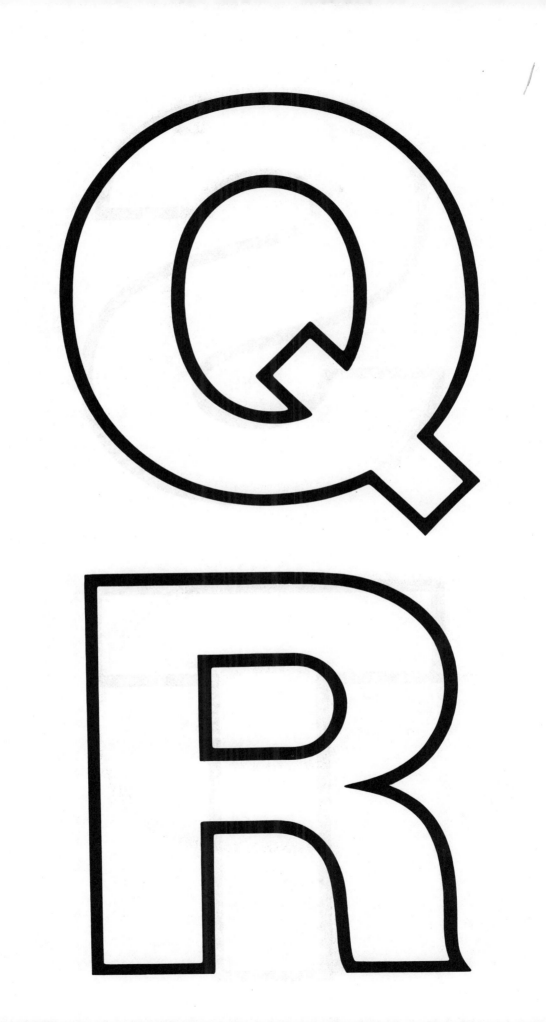

3

S

T

U

V

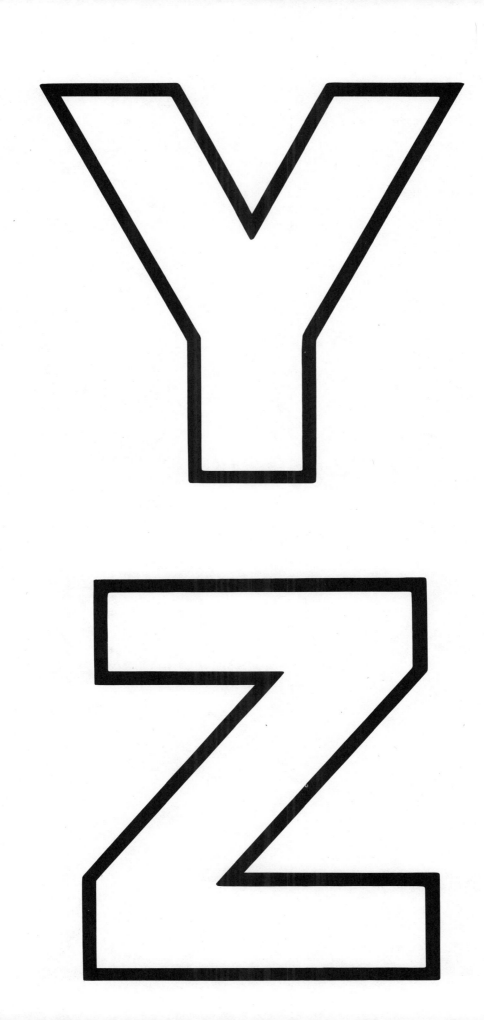

1

2

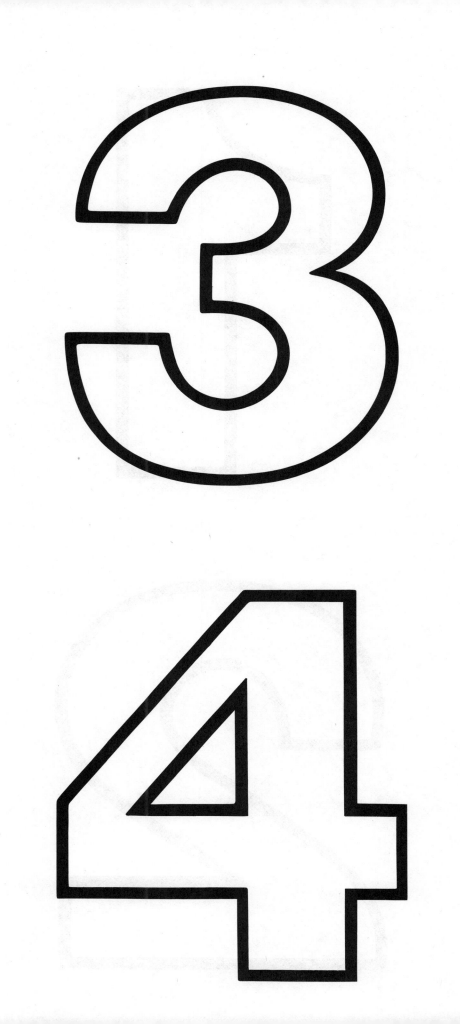

5

6

7

8

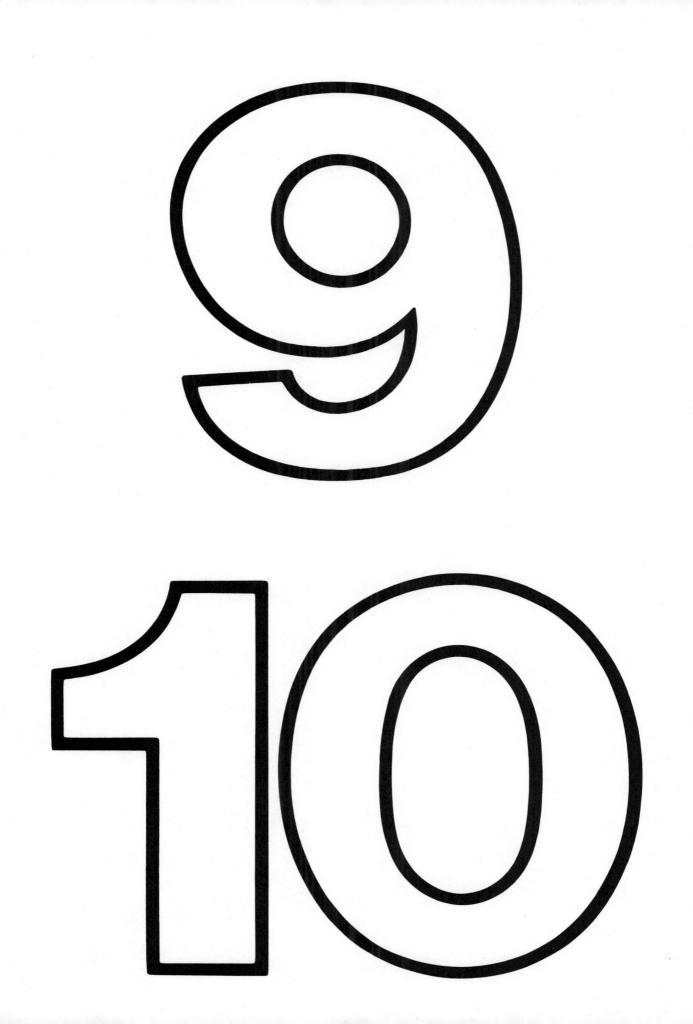